Scotland
the age of achievement

Cover. Waterloo Place from the east end of Princes Street, Edinburgh, engraved in 1825.

Scotland
the age of achievement

John Patrick

LECTURER IN HISTORY
ABERDEEN COLLEGE OF EDUCATION

John Murray London

Printed in Great Britain
by Butler & Tanner Ltd, Frome and London

0 7195 3273 6

Preface

This is intended primarily as a text book for 'O' grade students studying the Scottish History option in the alternative syllabus.

I have tried to include documentary material wherever possible, and if an undue amount of it seems to refer to Aberdeenshire, that is because I used what came most readily to hand. Teachers may like to correct this bias by research in their own areas. Eighteenth-century statistics are notoriously unreliable, and those which are quoted should be regarded only as a rough guide. I hope the questions at the end of each chapter will be looked on in a similar spirit. The best questions are those devised by the individual teacher for his own group.

I am indebted to my colleague Mr. Finlay McKichan and to Mr. Arthur McCombie, deputy Headmaster at Rubislaw Academy, Aberdeen, who read the manuscript and made several helpful suggestions. Two of Mr. McCombie's pupils, Graham Craig and Ian Carry, kindly pointed out various obscurities, which I have done my best to remove. I am solely to blame for the errors and omissions which remain. Mr. Raymond Johnstone helped me with the maps and Mrs. Sylvia Smith typed the manuscript. My thanks to all of them.

NOTE TO SECOND EDITION

For this new edition the chapter on the Highlands has been completely rewritten to take account of recent publications by Professor A. J. Youngson, Dr. Eric Richards and Mr. R. J. Adam. Slight changes have also been made to other chapters.

J.P.

Acknowledgments

A book of this sort depends largely on secondary works. I am pleased to acknowledge my debt to Dr. William Ferguson's *Scotland 1689 to the Present*, to Professor Roy Campbell's *Scotland since 1707*, to the late Professor Henry Hamilton's *Industrial Revolution in Scotland* and *Economic History of Scotland in the Eighteenth Century*, to Professor Christopher Smout's *History of the Scottish People*, to Mr. Malcolm Gray's *Highland Economy* and to Dr. Jean Lindsay's *Canals of Scotland*. Many other works have, of course, been consulted, but if any of the above had not been written this book would have been significantly different.

Thanks are due to the following who have kindly permitted the reproduction of copyright photographs:

Edinburgh University Library (pages 4, 39, 70, 147); Edinburgh Public Libraries (6, 61); British Museum (8, 19, 89); National Gallery of Scotland (27, 42, 131, 136, 146); Carron Company (44); Radio Times Hulton Picture Library (45, 93); David & Charles, from *Industrial History in Pictures—Scotland* by J. R. Hume (46); National Coal Board (48); Ronan Picture Library (73); Science Museum (78); Duke of Buccleuch (104); Scottish National Portrait Gallery (113, 125, 128, 143); Edinburgh University Library, from *Picturesque Views of Edinburgh* by J. W. Ewbank (cover).

Thanks are also due to: Dr. A. R. B. Haldane for permission to include the drove roads on the map on page 85 from *The Drove Roads of Scotland* (Edinburgh University Press (1968)); Oliver & Boyd for permission to redraw the illustrations on pages 15 and 22 from *Scottish Farming* by J. A. Symon; Keeper of the Records of Scotland for permission to redraw the illustrations on page 69 from *The Gordon Papers*; The Trustees of the National Library of Scotland for permission to quote from *The Melville Papers*; Council of Scottish History Society for permission to include extracts from *The Monymusk Papers* (ed. Henry Hamilton) and *Argyll Estate Instructions* (ed. Eric R. Cregeen).

Contents

Illustrations

Maps

A note on money

No attempt has been made to convert £.s.d. into decimal currency. This is because wages and prices have changed so much since the eighteenth century that it would be misleading to say that 1s was the equivalent of 5p. All £.s.d., unless marked 'Scots', is in sterling.

1 mark   =   13s 4d Scots
£1 Scots =   1s 8d Sterling

1 Introduction

The Scottish landowners

There was, according to Charles II in 1678, 'no nation or Kingdom in the world, where the tenants had so great a dependence upon the gentlemen as in Scotland'. No doubt this was an exaggeration, but it is certainly true that the landed gentry controlled almost every aspect of Scottish life in the seventeenth and early eighteenth centuries. Before the Act of Union they dominated the Scottish parliament, and after it they controlled the elections to the House of Commons. The same was true at a local level. Every landowner had his baron court before which he could call his tenants, and many of the nobility inherited important offices along with their titles. Thus the Duke of Hamilton was hereditary sheriff of Lanarkshire, while in the Highlands the clan chiefs had almost the powers of military commanders over their people. No matter what government was in power, these men ruled the areas in which they lived.

After the rebellion of 1745 some attempt was made to reduce the power of the Scottish nobility. In 1747 all inherited judicial posts were abolished, so that the government could now appoint sheriffs and justices of its own choice, and in the same year agreements which bound the tenants to fight for the landowner were ended. The baron courts, too, lost much of their power, and now dealt only with rent arrears and the like. None the less the gentry were still dominant. The sheriffs were chosen from among their number, as were the justices of the peace, on whose shoulders fell the burden of supervising the collection of taxes, resolving disputes between employers and their work people, and supervising the provision and repair of roads and bridges. In this last task they were helped by the commissioners of supply, again chosen from among the landowners. These commissioners had originally been appointed in every county to supervise the collection of the 'cess', land tax, but were now involved in the provision of roads, schools and prisons.

But even if he held none of these posts, the local landowner or heritor was a man of importance. In the eighteenth century the parish minister was usually nominated by a patron who was generally the head of the richest landowning family in the area. The heritors were also responsible for providing a school and paying the teacher in each parish, but, unlike their English counterparts, they did not normally have to support the poor of the parish. This was the responsibility of the church and there was rarely enough money to provide essentials for even the most deserving cases. Some money came from collections made at the church door, and from donations and legacies. A proportion of various rents and fees charged by the church went to swell the funds, and the fines levied by the kirk sessions were also used for this purpose. But if times were hard there was simply not enough to go round, and many resorted to begging, frequently leaving their own parish and making for the nearest town where they hoped there might be more money about. In 1774 a citizen of Aberdeen complained that 'the Inundations of Vagrant and Stranger Begging Poor for several Years past into Aberdeen from different Corners and Parishes almost exceed Belief', and the council introduced a system by which only those who had lived in the town for three years were allowed to beg. Non-resident beggars were to be committed to hard labour.

Harsh measures like this did not solve the problem, but one cannot help having some sympathy with the citizens of Aberdeen, who had financed and set up a hospital for their poor as early as 1741 and saw no reason why they should have to provide for those from the surrounding countryside as well. It was, in fact, open to every parish to levy a special poor rate if they chose, but this was very unpopular. In 1700 only three parishes had an assessment. By 1800 the number had grown to ninety-six, and by 1820 to two hundred and nine. This meant that even in 1820 more than three-quarters of the parishes of Scotland still relied principally on voluntary contributions to provide for their poor. This system was not modified until 1845, and was in marked contrast to that in England where poor rates were levied in every parish and, especially before 1834, were often a considerable burden on the landowner.

Clearly the Scottish gentry were privileged, and the richest of them lived a life which had little in common with that of their fellow-countrymen. Some, indeed, were not often in Scotland, except at election time, spending their time and money in London and having their children educated at English schools. Their estates were run for them by agents or factors. Others, however, were more down-to-earth. They lived on their estates and sent their sons to the local school. They were richer than their tenants, but mixed with them pretty freely. They knew well how hard life in eighteenth-century Scotland could be, for she was a backward country. She lacked industry. Her agriculture, though improving, was not up to the English standard. Travel was difficult if not dangerous, and over much of the country people lived in poverty in isolated communities. What towns there were excited the wonder rather than the admiration of an English visitor. What, for instance, was he to make of Edinburgh?

Scottish towns

The capital city consisted basically of a single street, stretching the mile and a quarter from Holyrood House to the Castle. Off it there ran numerous alleys and courts, with the buildings rising to ten or even twelve stories. Each block might contain within it a complete cross-section of society. The middle floors would be occupied by the upper classes—lawyers, professors, judges or even aristocrats. Above and below them lived tradesmen and, crowded into the attics and cellars, the ordinary working people. All used the same common stair, and on each dark landing stood the 'luggies' in which were kept the slops and filth from that particular flat. At 10 p.m. these were emptied into the street, which was cleared the next morning. This method of sewage disposal was the despair of visitors. 'How long can it be suffered,' wrote John Wesley in 1762, 'that all manner of filth should be flung into

CROSS at EDINBURGH.

Part of the old town of Edinburgh. The high tenements and narrow alleys may be seen on the right.

the streets? How long shall the capital city of Scotland and the chief street of it stink worse than a common sewer?'

Edinburgh was, indeed, in many ways a provincial rather than a capital city. However it did have Holyrood House, an untenanted royal palace tucked away at the foot of the hill, and halfway up there was the parliament building. Here justice was dispensed according to Scottish law by the judges of the Court of Session. They were learned men, but they sometimes lacked the dignity desirable in a judge. Their manner on the bench was often homely, and sometimes brutal. They and the lawyers spoke broad Scots, which grated on an English ear and made them almost incomprehensible if called on to plead a case before the House of Lords.

Life in Edinburgh was very public. Business deals were made in taverns over a drink of claret or brandy, and everybody in the cramped teeming town knew everybody else. It was a bustling, cheerful down-to-earth society, lacking gentility and polish and looking for leadership to London, where Scots with talent and ambition had a much better chance of making a name and a fortune than in Edinburgh. To London had gone all Scotland's politicians and the best of her business men, artists and imaginative writers. Most of her lawyers, trained in Scottish and not English law, stayed in Edinburgh. They made up the most important educated group in the capital. They were joined by a few scholars, for the university was a good one.

If Edinburgh was provincial, what of the other towns? Glasgow had a thriving tobacco trade with the plantations, and this had resulted in the growth of a class of wealthy merchants, who had built splendid houses with fine gardens on the outskirts of the town. These apart, most of Glasgow's buildings and those of other Scottish towns were cramped and insanitary, and the people who lived in them even more rough and ready than the inhabitants of Edinburgh. Only the prospect of a journey into the Scottish countryside could have induced the traveller to linger in most towns.

The countryside

All travellers condemned the barren, treeless wastes of Lowland Scotland. They wrote of wind-swept wildernesses, with wretched peasants clawing a bare living from a sour and ungrateful soil—if they were lucky. They condemned the frightful flea-ridden inns, and the tracks, alternately stony and muddy, which served as roads. Some bold spirits ventured into the Highlands. This was a great adventure, for they were now in the country where the rebellions of 1715 and 1745 had begun. True, the powers of the clan chiefs had been much reduced; some of the Highland estates had been taken over by the government and were being administered by the commissioners for forfeited estates; and all the arms in the Highlands were meant to have been collected and the wearing of the tartan kilt was forbidden. Yet even so, many felt insecure in this barbarian country whose dwellings were even more wretched than those in the Lowlands. The people looked wild, for they

This engraving of Burns's birthplace gives a fair idea of the standard of much rural housing and many rural roads towards the end of the eighteenth century.

were commonly dirty and ragged. They sounded wild, too, for they spoke Gaelic. They seemed, moreover, to regulate their lives according to a pattern which made little or no sense to outsiders. They refused to take any initiative or to work hard to improve their lot. And yet many of them had risked all to follow Charles Edward to Derby. In such company Edinburgh seemed indeed a metropolis of comfort and good manners. But it would take several days to get there from almost any part of the Highlands.

Relationships with England

Such impressions as these were taken back to England, and helped to harden the attitude of contempt with which most Englishmen regarded Scotland and Scotsmen. In the eighteenth century the Scot had to endure the same sort of suspicion and misrepresentation which today sometimes faces Commonwealth immigrants. All too often Scotsmen behaved as if they too believed themselves to be inferior. Edinburgh society flocked to be taught correct

English pronunciation by Thomas Sheridan, an Irishman. Tobias Smollett, a Scottish novelist who had sought and achieved fame in England, raised many an easy laugh by depicting his fellow-countrymen as simpletons or boastful idiots, and when the young James Boswell was introduced to Dr. Johnson in 1763, the first thing he did was to apologise for his nationality. 'Mr. Johnson,' he said, 'I do indeed come from Scotland, but I cannot help it.'

It is true that at subsequent meetings Boswell did much to try to raise Johnson's opinion of Scotland, and with some success. So far as education was concerned he was on pretty safe ground for, though Johnson would never admit it, Scotland had a better system of schools than did England, and her universities were certainly better. In two fields she had a clear lead. Adam Smith was the foremost political economist in Britain, while at Edinburgh David Hume and Principal Robertson (whose works sold well south of the border) were the best historians. Johnson disliked Scotland's Presbyterian religion, which was, in any case, a declining force, but admitted that Scottish law had good features. But, when hard-pressed, he could always turn the tables with a sneer at Scotland's poverty.

The beginnings of change

Yet there was wealth in Scotland. Some of the nobility had built splendid houses within easy reach of Edinburgh, and much of the money to do it came from improvements in farming, which resulted in greater productivity and higher rents. Glasgow was not the only place where new dwellings were being built. Visitors to Edinburgh noticed that a couple of elegant squares were being laid out to the south of the old town, while here and there up and down the country new village communities were being planned and built by improving landowners. It was a small beginning, but it heralded a revolution in Scotland's way of life, the dawn of a new confidence and prosperity.

Overleaf. Thurso, as laid out by Sir John Sinclair. Winding lanes were replaced by straight streets, with neat symmetrical blocks of buildings.

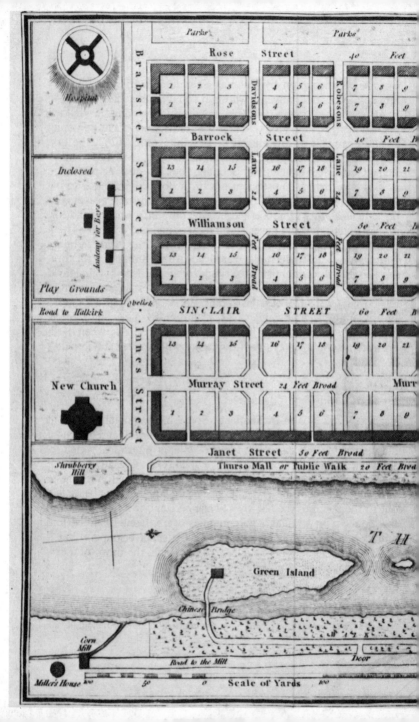

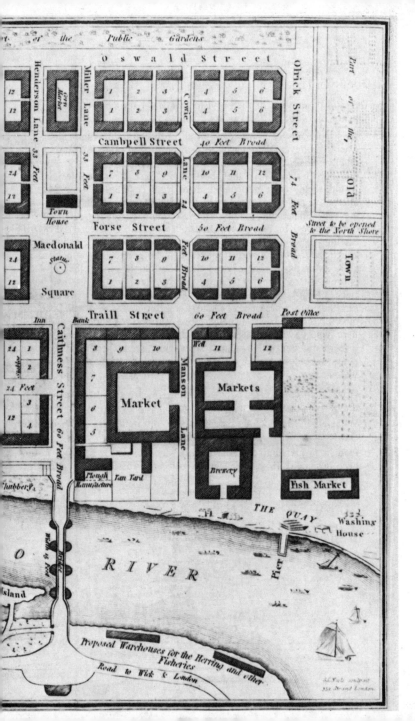

Document

This is a description of the provision made for the poor in the parish of Kiltearn in 1790:

> It is truly matter of regret, that no proper and effectual scheme has ever been devised among us to provide for the poor. At present they chiefly subsist by begging from door to door, not only in the respective parishes to which they belong, but over all the county; and it would seem hard to prohibit them from begging, as they have no alternative but to starve. The weekly collections made in the churches are very inadequate to the purpose of supporting the poor in any of our parishes. In this parish, the collections never exceed £8 or £10 Sterling yearly. About £6 arises from charitable mortifications, which, added to the above, makes the whole fund for the poor about £15. After paying the session-clerk, and some other officers of the church, there remains about £10 Sterling, which is distributed once a year among the most indigent persons of the parish by the kirk-session, in presence of the heritors. But how small a relief can this afford, when there are usually above 100 persons upon the poor's list here, who have every claim to charity that indigence and infirmity can give them? nor will it appear surprising that the poor's roll in this place should be so large, when it is recollected that there are 96 widows in it.

a How much could each poor person in Kiltearn expect to receive from the parish poor funds, according to the figures given by the minister?
b What other disadvantages were there in the system as outlined in the extract?
c Had 'a proper and effectual scheme' to provide for the poor in fact been designed? If so, what was it, and why was it not put into effect everywhere?

2 Agriculture in the Lowlands

Scottish agriculture was traditionally backward. The country was admittedly hard to farm. Of a total of 19 000 000 acres, less than 5 000 000 were fit for cultivation, the rest being moss, mountain and moor. Much of the soil was thin and acid. The climate, with excessive rainfall in some places and treacherously late and early frosts in others, made it difficult to grow some crops at all or to rely on the yield of any. There were, then, natural disadvantages which were, however, magnified by the system of farming adopted over most of the country.

The old system

Organisation

The traditional early eighteenth-century farm had about three hundred and fifty acres. Several families would work it, paying rent to the laird who owned the land. The farm would be divided into three sections. That nearest the dwellings was called the infield, and consisted of the richest soil. Surrounding it was the outfield, larger in area, but much poorer. Outside that, sometimes divided from it by a dyke, lay an area of pasture, usually very rough and rocky. Of all this land, only the infield, which might consist of about twenty acres, and about twenty acres of the outfield were cultivated at any one time. All the cultivated land was divided up into strips or ridges, between two hundred and five hundred yards long and about ten or fifteen yards wide, separated by balks of

View from the outskirts of Elgin in 1693. The town is at the top. In the middle distance there is a water mill. The division of the land into rigs can be clearly seen.

earth covered with grass, bracken and bramble. These strips were distributed among the various tenants, usually being reallocated every year or perhaps every two or three years, rarely less frequently. Thus no tenant ever held the land long enough to make it worth his while to spend time, energy or money on improving it. The strips of the infield were under continuous cultivation. A third of the land was manured with animal dung, the thatch of houses, and sometimes the scourings from ditches. It was then sown with 'bere', a type of barley. The rest of the infield, unmanured, was sown with oats. The next year another section was manured and sown with bere and so on. Thus the infield was always under a corn crop—one year bere, followed by two years of oats. The return was scanty; three or four grains for every one that was sown was considered satisfactory.

This crop was supplemented by the produce of the outfield, about half of which was cultivated. Usually a section of it was sown with oats for about five years continuously until the crop barely gave back the amount of grain that was sown. Then the land was left under grass for a few years to recover, while another section was ploughed and sown. The remainder of the outfield, together with the pasture, had to support the livestock of the farm —horses, cattle, sheep, hens. It was rarely sufficient.

So much for the system in outline. It was not universal. In a few places there were enclosed fields, in others the rotation of crops was different, including peas and beans. But over most of the country, the principles were the same—the division of land into strips, known as 'run-rig', the continuously cropped infield, the partially cropped outfield and the thin, sour pasture. This was bad enough, but there were other things which made matters even worse. In the first place the strains of both crops and animals were inferior. In many parts grey oats were still grown. These, although very hardy, were light and unproductive. Slowly they were being replaced by the much heavier-cropping white oats, especially on the infield. The grey oats, which excited sneers and contempt from farmers from other lands, were, until the end of the eighteenth century, still grown on the outfield in the Highlands, mainly for fodder. Bere, too, was not as productive as other sorts of barley, though it withstood the wet climate well, and matured early. No special grasses were sown—pasture simply consisted of whatever happened to grow wild on the spot.

Livestock

This meant that the animals, like the crops, had to be good survivors rather than good producers. Thus the cattle were lean and hardy, so ill-fed that they often calved only every two years. They weighed only about three hundredweight, except in Galloway where grazing conditions were much better and they often reached five or six hundredweight. In spring they wandered about the farmstead at will until seed time, and were then confined to the outfield or the moorland pasture. For a couple of hours in the middle of the day and again at night they were put into folds on the outfield, where they were fed with thistles. After the harvest they were allowed again to wander at will, existing through the winter on straw, chaff, dry rushes, coarse dried grass and a few oats. In the spring they were frequently so weak they had to be carried from the byres to the pasture to graze. The sheep were similarly stunted, weighing about ten pounds a quarter—in the Highlands less. The moorland pasture was burned off in early spring to encourage the growth of grass, and the sheep turned on to it. The ewes were commonly milked after lambing, and were often kept in at night to protect them from wild cats. To keep them free from vermin they were smeared with a mixture of tar and butter, which ruined their fleeces. Competing with them and the cattle were the horses, which were frequently tethered on to the balks or else driven out on to the pasture. In winter they ate straw, or whatever they could scrape up from the soil with their hooves. They were therefore weak and undersized and unable to do much work. This meant that to provide the necessary power for the farm, a large number had to be kept. This meant that there was insufficient fodder, so they were weak and undersized. There seemed no way out of the vicious circle. Many farmers had no horses and used slow and clumsy oxen instead.

Implements

Farm implements were no better than the livestock. The Scottish plough was a huge clumsy wooden contrivance. It was difficult to get it to cut a clean furrow, and the friction was enormous. It needed the strength of eight or ten oxen to drag it through the ground and four men had to supplement the animals' efforts. One walked with the animals, one at the nose of the plough to keep it straight, a third held the shafts of the plough while the last followed behind to break up any lumps still remaining. Breakdowns and stoppages were frequent, and the team was satisfied to plough half an acre a day. On light upland soils a lighter plough was used, but it was not very effective. The harrow was a wooden frame, about four feet square, set with wooden teeth which frequently broke. It was so light that it was sometimes tied to the tail of the horse which was pulling it. It was therefore of little use on really heavy soil. A saw-tooth sickle was used to cut the grain and a bunch of heather frequently served as a flail.

Country society

So primitive a system of farming could produce little wealth. In fact it sometimes failed to provide the minimum necessary to feed the population. The last years of the seventeenth century had seen a famine in Scotland, and even after 1750 there were still years when there was real want. At best there was poverty, not only for the tenant farmer, but even for the landowner. Rents were often paid partly in produce and labour, which meant that the laird accumulated huge quantities of inferior grain and stringy hens while his land was cultivated by tenants who begrudged the time spent away from their own rigs. To get rid of the meal and the hens, the landowner paid as many salaries as he could in kind, and entertained visitors without stint. But this was making the best of a bad job. He would have preferred cash rents, to spend as he thought fit.

The tenant was much worse off. His farmhouse was usually made of loose, undressed stone with the gaps between filled in with clay or turfs. The roof was composed of a thatch of rushes, ferns and heather and was renewed every year. The floor was earth, and the stone fireplace was in the centre of the floor. There was no chimney, and artificial light was provided by a piece of bog fir, or a fish-oil lamp. Animals and humans were under the same roof, and furniture was of the crudest kind. The house can never have been really dry or clean, which encouraged disease. Nor was the diet satisfactory, being based on oatmeal, with meat only when an

This type of plough was much used in the north-east of Scotland in the eighteenth century. It needed twelve oxen to pull it.

Abstract rent roll of Monymusk, crop. 1733

				Sterg. Money		
				£	s	d
To Money Rent of Mony^{k} & Pitfiechy				266	12	4
To Money for Converted Bear				26	15	$5\frac{1}{2}$
To Money for Converted Meal				5	11	$1\frac{1}{3}$
To 11 bolls 1 fir. Horse Corn with straw,		s	d			
per Boll	@	6	8	3	18	$1\frac{1}{3}$
To $16\frac{1}{2}$ Leit of Peats	@	8	4	6	17	6
To $13\frac{1}{2}$ do.	@	6	8	4	10	0
To $358\frac{1}{2}$ Capons	@	0	5	7	19	$4\frac{1}{2}$
To $627\frac{1}{2}$ Hens	@	0	3	7	16	$10\frac{1}{2}$
To $56\frac{1}{2}$ Geese	@	1	$1\frac{1}{3}$	3	2	$9\frac{1}{3}$
To $20\frac{1}{2}$ Wedders	@	4	2	4	5	5
To 1 Lamb				0	1	8
To 5 Mill Swine	@	11	$1\frac{1}{3}$	2	15	$6\frac{2}{3}$
To $2\frac{1}{2}$ Stones of Butter	@	5	4	0	13	4
To 8 Haggs of Sheep	@	3	4	1	6	8
To $134\frac{3}{4}$ Hesps of Linen Yarn	@	0	$6\frac{2}{3}$	3	14	$10\frac{2}{3}$
To 1 Ston of Tallow				0	5	4
To 84 Chickens	@	0	$1\frac{1}{2}$	0	10	6
To 830 bolls, 1 fir; 1 peck of Meal	@	6	$11\frac{1}{3}$	288	8	6
To 150 bolls, 2 fir; $\frac{1}{3}$ of a peck of Bear	@	6	$11\frac{1}{3}$	52	5	3
				£686	17	$7\frac{2}{3}$

Deduct from the Above

				£	s	d			
To the Minister of Monymusk of Money Stipend				25	0	0			
To do. 26 bolls of Meal		s	d						
cond.	@	6	$11\frac{1}{3}$	9	0	$6\frac{2}{3}$			
To do. 13 bolls of Bear	@	6	$11\frac{1}{3}$	4	10	$3\frac{1}{3}$			
To Minister of Chappel of Money Stipend				0	11	$0\frac{1}{2}$			
To do. 3 pecks of Meal	@	6	$11\frac{1}{3}$	0	1	$3\frac{1}{2}$			
To Minister of Oyne of Money				9	15	$3\frac{1}{3}$			
To do. 1 boll of 2 fir: of meal	@	6	$11\frac{1}{3}$	0	10	5			
To School Master of Oyne				0	10	5			
To do. $1\frac{1}{2}$ peck of Meal		6	$11\frac{1}{3}$	0	0	$7\frac{2}{3}$			
To the Chappel Royal of Few				4	4	6			
To the Arch Bishop of St. Andrews of do.				4	15	$2\frac{2}{3}$			
To the Duke of Gordon of do.				6	1	3	55	11	$0\frac{1}{2}$
							£631	6	$7\frac{1}{6}$

N.B.—There is 29 bolls of Meal and 2 bolls of Bear of additional rent at the expiration of the present tacks, and between £20 and £25 sterg. of additional rent on the expiration of the tacks of the mills, besides some ground in nurseries, etc. not rented with the Gardens of Mony^{k} & Paradise and all the ground upon which the planting grew.

This is the Rent Roll by Which I have accounted.

THOS. WILSON.

animal died. The only fresh vegetable was cabbage, which was grown in the kail-yard near the house. There was little enough of this, and scurvy was by no means uncommon. Beer was the usual drink among tenants. The laird had whisky.

But even the tenant farmer had labourers. Some, known as 'cottars', had their own cottages with an acre of ground to work and the right to pasture a cow in return for working for the tenant. Others lived on the farm or in the adjoining bothy, and were paid wages in cash or kind. A chief ploughman might expect £2 sterling a year—an unskilled labourer only half that sum in addition to board, lodging and cloth. Maidservants and boys were paid about 10s a year.

Comparison with England

The returns from farming in Scotland compared very badly with those in England. The traditional English three-field system, where each year a third of the arable land was left fallow without a crop, took less out of the soil than did the more intensive Scottish system. Yet even this was being abandoned in England in favour of enclosed fields and new crop rotations, while selective breeding and proper feeding were helping to produce better strains of livestock. Agricultural improvement became all the rage. About 1730 Viscount Townshend took time off from a distinguished political career to concentrate on improving his estates, while later in the century Thomas Coke of Holkham increased his rents from £2000 to £20 000 a year by better farming methods.

Such achievements did not pass unnoticed in Scotland. Through the years many gentry travelled across England and could not fail to see and to hear of new farming methods which made Scottish farming seem prehistoric by comparison. They came back to Scotland determined to catch up. From the legal point of view there were few difficulties. In England the three-field system contained so complex a mass of individual rights that it required a separate act of parliament to dismantle it on each estate. In Scotland, if the proprietors

Opposite. This account shows how the rents on the Monymusk Estate were partly payable in grain and animals, which were all given a cash value.

of the land decided to reorganise their estates, an act of 1695 made it possible without further formality. The short leases could now be turned to advantage, for as soon as they fell in, the tenants could be turned off, the rigs divided up into enclosed fields and redistributed on long leases to tenants who were expected, often as a condition of the lease, to employ new techniques and crops. At first the changes had to be financed by the landowner—fortunately the supply of cash and capital available in Scotland increased after the Union. Gradually, however, as the returns increased, so the rents were to be raised, so that tenant and laird would both become more prosperous.

In fact there were many difficulties to be overcome. In the first place some crop rotations suitable in England were impracticable in Scotland and required substantial modification. For instance many places in Scotland were unsuitable for growing wheat. Nor did some strains of cattle do well. Next, it was often difficult to get the tenants to change their ways. Some merely disliked change. Others suspected that they were simply being used as a means to make the laird richer without corresponding benefit to themselves. Finally—and most important—the whole process of agricultural improvement took much longer than many had calculated. The terrain was so rough, the climate so hard, the soil so impoverished that in some cases the estate swallowed up all the resources the landowner could put into it and still demanded more before producing a really worthwhile return on the money he invested. In Aberdeenshire, for instance, clearing, draining and planting the land could cost anything up to £100 an acre and little more than £4 a year could be expected from it in rent. Thus bankruptcies among improvers were not unknown, but the persevering got their reward.

Improvements in the Lothians

The earliest improvements were made in the Lothians. By the time of his death in 1735 the sixth Earl of Haddington had enclosed his old run-rig farms, introduced clover as a farm crop, sowed special grasses and planted three hundred acres of timber, but his efforts paled into insignificance when compared with those of John

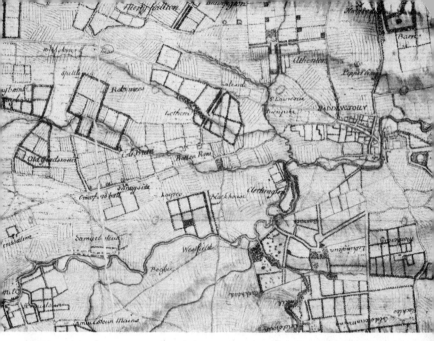

The Haddington area, mapped by Roy in about 1750, was in the process of being improved. One can see the newly enclosed fields side by side with the old-style rigs.

Cockburn of Ormiston. Born in 1679, he had sat in the last Scottish parliament, and was an MP at Westminster from 1707 to 1741. He brought in improving tenant farmers from England to whom he gave long leases on the farms whose fields he had enclosed from the old run-rig. He encouraged his Scottish tenants to grow wheat, turnips and grasses in addition to their traditional crops. The grasses were made into hay and provided, together with the turnips, winter food for the livestock, whose weight, health and strength were vastly increased. Cockburn constantly bustled about his estates, supervising, advising, persuading and bullying. Even when he was in London he wrote and received a detailed and voluminous correspondence about the progress on his farms. He founded an Agricultural Society in 1736 which met every month in the village inn. He rebuilt Ormiston village, setting up a brewery and a distillery to use the barley from the estate farms. He sent his tenants' sons to England to learn the latest farming methods, and

19

taught their daughters to spin. In 1745 he rebuilt Ormiston House, but in 1748 he went bankrupt and had to sell out to the Earl of Hopetoun.

Societies and books

Cockburn was a prominent member of the Society for Improving in the Knowledge of Agriculture, established in Edinburgh in 1723. Its members were nobility and gentry who met every three months to discuss the latest agricultural methods. The society also published essays for the benefit of non-members, and though it seems to have died out about 1745 its example was widely followed, so that from 1730 onwards there was an ever-increasing flow of pamphlets and books available to those who wished to improve their land. All condemned run-rig and attacked the planting of two grain crops in succession. The earlier works tended to recommend a fallow year on arable land, but later more emphasis was placed on growing turnips and clover and sowing specially selected grasses for hay. All recommended tree-planting as a way of protecting farm and fields against the worst of the weather, while at the same time providing, in the long term, a valuable cash-crop.

Typical of such authors was Robert Maxwell of Arkland in Dumfriesshire, the secretary of the society. Born in 1695, he farmed a hundred and thirty acres at Clifton Hall near Edinburgh, held on a long lease. He experimented on his own farm and supervised improvements on landowners' estates. He was the probable author of a treatise concerning the manner of fallowing written in 1724, and in 1743 he published the various queries which had been addressed to the society together with the answers which had been given. In 1750 he had to give up farming because of financial difficulties and became a full-time adviser. In 1756 he lectured in Edinburgh on agriculture and in 1757 published *The Practical Husbandman*. Almost up to his death in 1765 he remained an energetic advocate of new methods of farming, carrying on a voluminous correspondence.

By 1760 so much had been written that it seemed time to draw it all together in one work. This was done by Adam Dickson, a minister of Duns in Berwickshire. In 1762 the first volume of his *Treatise on Agriculture* appeared. The second volume was published in 1769. So popular was this 2000-page treatise that new editions were brought out in 1770 and 1785. A different kind of work was produced by Andrew Wight, who farmed on Cockburn's old estates at Ormiston. Between 1778 and 1784 he published four volumes on *The Present State of Husbandry in Scotland*. In this he surveyed the agricultural scene all over the country, beginning with the work being done on the forfeited estates, and paying most attention to improvers.

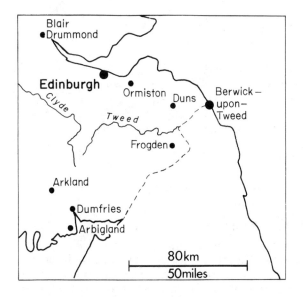

Improvers in the South

Meanwhile other farmers in the south and west of the country had been attracting attention. In Kirkcudbright William Craig of Arbigland, who died in 1798, had cleared his land of weeds and stones, introduced new crop rotations, designed better farming implements, imported some of the improved strains of sheep and cattle bred by Bakewell in Leicestershire and taken in pupils to spread and perpetuate his ideas. In Roxburghshire William Dawson, who took over the tenancy of Frogden in 1759, spent much time and money draining his land. He counteracted the acidity of the soil by applying quantities of lime. For winter fodder he sowed turnips, using a seed-drill on specially ploughed land. His animals grew fatter, and their dung enriched his soil. In spite of paying increased rents he grew rich, which encouraged the other tenant farmers to follow his example without any pressure from the landlord.

The famous chain plough designed by James Small.

Kames and Small

Further north conditions were often more difficult. For instance, when Lord Kames, at the age of seventy, inherited the Blair Drummond estate in 1766, he found that 1500 acres of it were peat bog, while the remainder lacked roads and was poorly farmed. He set to work with an imagination and energy which would have done credit to a man half his age. He paid nearly half the cost of a bridge across the Forth to make it easier to bring lime to his estates and he organised the statute labour to improve the roads. He enclosed fields and cleared them of stones. He encouraged his tenants to grow green as well as corn crops and to sow grass seed.

He also gave them better ploughs, like that designed by James Small of Berwickshire. It made a clean cut and produced a wide furrow. Parts of it were made of iron, which meant it was better shaped and lasted longer. It generated much less friction, and required only a quarter of the number of horses to do twice the work. It was most suitable for well-worked soil, and as better methods of cultivation spread, so Small's plough became more and more useful. He publicised it in a book written in 1784. At about the same time Andrew Meikle was designing a threshing machine which appeared in 1786. It could be driven by water, horse or steam power and was much used on large farms. It was unpopular among labourers because it reduced the demand for workers in the winter.

Kames's main task was to clear the great moss of Kincardine which covered the fertile soil by a depth of anything up to twelve feet. This was done by digging channels, and floating the peat off down the Forth. A water wheel was employed to fill a pool behind a sluice which was opened at intervals to give a better flow of water to sweep the moss away. To get tenants to take on the task of clearing he offered them leases of thirty-eight years, the first seven of which were rent free. Indeed Kames even went so far as to offer free meal and timber while they were building their houses. After seven years a nominal rent was charged, gradually increasing until after nineteen years they were paying 12s an acre for land which had been cleared, and still only 2s 6d for uncleared land. Kames must have known that he would never live to reap any financial reward from what he had undertaken—he in fact died in 1782. He was an enthusiastic and far-sighted improver who seems to have worked for the joy of it. He tried to spread his ideas by publishing in 1776 *The Gentleman Farmer*, a book full of good advice.

Not that Kames was the only improver to undertake large-scale engineering works; John, Earl of Strathmore from 1737 to 1776, drained the Loch of Forfar to get at the shell marl on its bottom. Unlike Kames, he was able to make £1000 a year by selling this mixture of mud and lime, but he also offered his tenants long leases on enclosed land and did much to improve the breed of cattle.

Improvers in the North-East

The North-East, too, had its pioneers. The earliest was probably Sir Archibald Grant of Monymusk, who took over his estates in 1716. His energy and originality were prodigious. He enclosed the run-rig and introduced crop rotation, encouraging his tenants to grow new crops like wheat and potatoes, while his own garden grew such exotic vegetables as onions, leeks and lettuce. He preached the value of liming and manuring the land and gave good farmers long leases on advantageous terms so long as they improved their land and introduced crop rotation. He used his baron court to enforce his wishes and to protect his trees—he is said to have planted 50 000 000 on his estates—from those tenants who took the leading shoots of young saplings to use to drive their oxen. In other respects he was a model landowner. He set up a lint mill and a saw mill and encouraged the growth of the cloth industry. Useful craftsmen, such as coopers and wheelwrights, were given training and premises, and stone polishing was introduced to try to bring a new occupation to his estates.

Sir Archibald's work increased the produce from his estates and consequently their value. Neighbouring lairds visited him and, seeing that the new methods worked even in Aberdeenshire, set out to try them themselves. About 1760 a farming club was set up at Gordon's mill in Aberdeen. It had fifteen members, six of whom were professors from the universities in Aberdeen. Its members organised expeditions and enquiries to find out exactly what was wrong with current agricultural practice, and then discussed how to put things right. The club sometimes initiated experiments in its own right but not as often as it would have liked. It was invaluable as a centre for discussion and information for local landowners, and its existence must have had something to do with the outstanding record of land improvement in the North-East in the second half of the eighteenth century.

In Banffshire, for instance, Lord Deskford, who succeeded to the title of Earl of Findlater in 1764, abolished run-rig on all his estates and introduced English crop rotation. He sent some of his tenants to study the work being done by Kames, and encouraged tradesmen to go to Edinburgh to improve their skills. He sent his estate factor on a tour to pick up useful ideas from others. Perhaps inspired by Sir Archibald Grant, he planted 11 000 000 trees on his estates and tried to encourage local industry. In Aberdeenshire Udny of Udny, as well as reclaiming and enclosing land, brought in shorthorn cattle from the borders. He invented a cheap turnip-sowing machine, but the best work on his estate was done by J. Anderson, whom Udny brought from the Lothians to take over a farm of more than 1000 acres at Monkshill.

But perhaps the most impressive pioneering work was done on two Kincardineshire estates. Robert Barclay inherited 3000 acres at Ury in 1760. They were not an inviting prospect. The estate was divided into small unprofitable farms and the soil was thin and sour. Few of the fields were flat and all were poorly drained. many with springs in the middle of them. Stones and boulders lay everywhere, making all farming operations difficult. Much of the land was, indeed, a marshy, heathery waste. Barclay was not discouraged. As the short leases on the farms near his mansion fell in, he took them over himself and set about making good farming land. The stones were cleared and disposed of. Some were heaped in the hollows and covered with earth. Some were used to make drains or line ditches. Others were made into walls or heaped into the corners of fields. More stones went into eight miles of roads which Barclay made on the estate, but there were still plenty left. In all 100 000 tons of stones had to be moved: some picked up, some grubbed out, large boulders being blasted to pieces with gunpowder.

Once the land was cleared, walled and drained it was ploughed or even trenched and then sweetened with generous applications of lime. Labourers imported from Norfolk brought in new crop rotations, and the pasture was so improved by manuring and seeding that Barclay could let it profitably to cattle graziers. Even the river banks and hillsides were turned to profit by being planted with trees. Over nine hundred acres were improved. The work paid off, and Barclay's tenants began to copy him. They were encouraged by long leases and had stone farmhouses built for them. As the land improved, the rents were raised and the rent roll, which had stood at £200 in 1760, had increased to £1600 by Barclay's death in 1797. It was no wonder that the farming club at Gordon's mill took a strong interest in the Ury estate. So did his neighbour, Silver, who, in 1754, after a career in the West Indies, had bought the estate of Netherley which was similar to that of Ury. The same pioneering work was carried out, though on a smaller scale. The example spread and farmers in the North-East cleared their fields of stones, stacking them in great heaps which can still be seen today, limed the soil, sowed new crops and reaped profits.

Sinclair of Ulbster

But the greatest figure of the agricultural revival in Scotland, Sir John Sinclair of Ulbster, came from Caithness. He was certainly as energetic as any, and was the only one to achieve a reputation throughout the United Kingdom. Educated at Edinburgh,

Glasgow, Oxford and Lincoln's Inn, he became MP for his county in 1780 at the age of twenty-six. He had already made a reputation for himself locally nearly ten years before by organising a gang of 1200 men to make a road across Ben Chielt in one day. He could never resist a challenge and loved to accumulate, organise and broadcast information. He lacked humour and sometimes seemed

Sir John Sinclair was clearly seen by Raeburn as a splendid Highland chieftain.

pompous, but he was very thorough and hard-working. He was, moreover, honest and, in spite of occasional quarrels, established himself with Prime Minister Pitt as a useful man who could be trusted.

To begin with he travelled widely, studying economics. He was not at first much interested in agriculture, but when once he took up improving, he did so in a big way. He believed in the virtues of sheep farming and on one part of his estate moved the entire population to the coast where he set up fisheries for them, gave them two Scottish acres each, and guaranteed them three hundred days work a year. In their place he introduced the Cheviot sheep with English shepherds. The income from this part of his estates rose from £300 to £1200 a year. It was, as we shall see, a lesson which was not lost on the Highland landowners. Not content with the Cheviot sheep, Sinclair founded the British Wool Society in 1791. Under its auspices he tried cross-breeding various strains of sheep, and brought the Shetland sheep to the mainland of Scotland. He thought its fine wool would be an asset. None of his cross-breeding really worked, and the Shetland sheep, used to rough, poor pasture, died on the rich fields of Caithness. The society was wound up in 1794.

But by this time Sinclair had plenty more to occupy him. He was impatient at the lack of available information about Scotland, information which he thought essential if the government were to be able to plan the nation's future properly. In 1790 he therefore organised a nation-wide survey to fill the gap. He had a circular letter printed and sent to every one of the nine hundred parish ministers in Scotland asking them to send an account of the parishes which they served. He asked for details of history, population, crops, work available, wages and prices. As the replies came in they were edited and, when there were enough to make a volume, printed and published. The first volume came out in 1791, but Sinclair had to send some ministers no fewer than twenty circulars before they would send in their reports. It was 1797 before the last of them had come in, and the twenty-first volume which completed Sinclair's *Statistical Account of Scotland* did not appear until 1799. The account is, of course, uneven in quality, since it depended entirely on the effort that each minister was

Labourer's budget in Auchterderran, 1790

Annual earnings of a day-labourer, his wife, and three children;
deducting four weeks earnings of the man on account of holidays,
bad health, attendance on funerals, etc. and excessive bad weather;
and four weeks earnings of the woman, on account of holidays, bad
health, and lying-in.

	£	s	d
To 48 weeks labour of a man at 1s a day	14	8	0
To 48 weeks labour of a woman, in spinning, besides taking care of her house and children	3	12	0
To the earnings of 3 children at the age of six, seven, and eight years, nothing			
	£18	**0**	**0**

Annual expence of a day-labourer, his wife and three children.

	£	s	d
By 2 pecks oat-meal a week, at 11½d per peck	4	19	8
By 2 pecks barley or pease-meal a week, at 7½d a peck	3	5	0
By 6 bolls potatoes, at 5s a boll	1	10	0
By barley for kail, at 3lb a week	0	16	3
By a kail-yard, and a wretched house	0	13	0
By milk, at 4d a week	0	17	4
By salt, cheese, and butter	0	12	6
By soap for washing clothes	0	2	6
By coals in a year, with carriage	1	0	0
By shoes to the whole family	1	0	0
By body-clothes to the man	1	10	0
By ditto to the woman and children	1	5	0
By worsted thread for mendings	0	7	0
	£17	**18**	**3**

This table, which comes from the *Statistical Account*, gives an idea of the
standard of living of an agricultural labourer in Fife.

prepared to put into his report. Some are full, painstaking and clear. Others are slapdash. But it remains a work of enormous interest and value, a splendid tribute to Sinclair's energy and persistence.

While the work on the *Statistical Account* was going on, Sinclair was involved in another pioneer venture. In 1793, in return for help in a financial crisis, he persuaded Pitt to set up a Board of Agriculture to centralise ideas and information about farming. Arthur Young was the secretary, with Sinclair himself as president and driving force. He soon upset his fellow members—and the government—by his desire to run the board entirely himself and frightened them by the expensive nature of the surveys he proposed. He was turned out in 1798, but got the job back for a further nine years in 1805. He at once set in hand a report, county by county, of agriculture throughout the country and in 1814 he was able, in addition, to bring out a *General Report on Scottish Agriculture*. This, as well as describing existing practices, contained proposals for future action. He had really wanted to cover England as well, but the board had not the resources. Scotland had already been well served by the volume he had published in 1812 on Scottish husbandry, and was to be put further in his debt by the *Analysis of the Statistical Account* which he published in 1826. He also wrote a *Code of Agriculture*, published in 1817, which tried to sum up all existing knowledge on the subject. (His attempt to do the same for health in 1809 had excited widespread ridicule.) All this was in addition to a constant stream of pamphlets and letters full of advice, usually unasked for and unwanted, to all manner of people on all manner of subjects.

Nor were his estates neglected. The fields were walled in, farmhouses, cottages and outbuildings were built. Roads and bridges were made and tenants attracted by long leases and low rents. Even the town of Thurso was rebuilt to Sinclair's design. Typically, he over-estimated the return on the money he had invested in his estates and in 1811, when he failed to get a legacy he had been expecting, he went bankrupt with debts of £50 000. This led to his retirement from parliament, but by his death in 1835 he was once again solvent. Though he tended to under-estimate the difficulties confronting him he remains one of the greatest collectors and organisers of information of his day. Historians will always be in his debt. Much of this chapter could not have been written without the information he provided.

Results of improvement

So much for the work of individual improvers. There were, of course, many more than have been mentioned in this chapter, for by 1820 the whole face of Scotland was being transformed. The pace of change was quickest after 1790, for the war against France which began in 1793 saw an increase in the price of grain. In 1794 wheat stood at 50s a quarter. In 1796 it fetched 96s, and in 1812 126s 6d. Other grain prices increased in proportion. Farmers therefore had more money to spend on improvements, and a better return on money which they spent. It is true that costs were rising as well. In 1792 it was reckoned that the total rental of the country stood at about £2 000 000. By 1812 it had risen to £5 000 000. Moreover, between 1750 and 1820 food prices doubled, or more than doubled, but labourers' pay more than kept pace with this. There is no doubt that during the war years Scottish agriculture paid good dividends, and prudent men made money. Those who lost their heads sometimes offered ridiculously high rents for farms, or paid out huge sums in bringing into cultivation very poor land whose produce could never justify the expense involved. Others, rejoicing at the high price of grain, tended to revert to the old Scottish practice of growing several corn crops in succession, thus exhausting the soil. For them the day of reckoning came after 1815 when the war ended and prices began to fall.

In fact Scottish farmers stood up to this test remarkably well, better than many in England. True, in England the poor rates were much higher than in Scotland, but the fact remains that Scottish farmers proved more adaptable. The great Lothian farms, with their factory-like buildings and steam threshing machines, could produce wheat as cheap as any in England. In less favoured areas, however, wheat was abandoned in favour of oats for the yield was more reliable in Scotland and the price more stable. Sheep were still profitable in Scotland, even when the prices dropped to half their peak, and so were cattle, especially on the lush pastures of the South-West. Thus improving was still going on, with new land being brought into cultivation well into the nineteenth century.

This revolution in farming left its mark on the countryside and on the people. Walled fields replaced the sprawling rigs, and slated stone farmhouses with outbuildings for the animals and cottages for the labourers were now commonplace. Towns, too, benefited. Many, like Thurso, were laid out afresh in the late eighteenth and early nineteenth centuries, often on a grid-iron pattern with a central square. Such improvements were usually financed by the profits from farming. So, too, were many of the new roads, and at least one canal. The people were better fed. They now had fresh meat, turnips and potatoes in addition to their traditional meal and cabbage. They began to take dry houses, substantial furniture and good clothes for granted, conscious that they were second to none where agricultural efficiency was concerned. Let us hope that they spared a thought for those who had fallen by the wayside, unable to adapt quickly enough to the new methods. Some had been squeezed out by higher rents which they could no longer afford. Many went to the industrial towns; others to the colonies. They made little mark, but their failure and despair were just as real as, were the confidence and success of men like Barclay and Grant.

Documents

1

In April 1774 the *Aberdeen Journal* published part of a letter written by a man about to emigrate:

> There is not a tract of better cultivated land in Scotland, considering the soil and opportunities we have than what we propose to leave; and no doubt it is a grief to our spirits to leave it and our native land; and venture upon such a dangerous voyage; but there is no help for it; we are not able to stand the high rents, and must do something for bread or see our families reduced to beggary.

Continue this letter in your own words, describing the course of events which led up to the rise in rent on the estate on which you lived.

2

In May 1774 the *Aberdeen Journal* published the following advertisement:

> Notice that any Nobleman or Gentleman who wants a proper qualified Grieve to manage a Farm, may write to George Vintner in Portsoy, where there is one just now. This man was born in the County of Northumberland and has been his whole lifetime employed in managing large Farms and improving Ground both in England and Scotland and has a thorough Knowledge in breeding Horses and Cattle likewise in fattening Cattle. If no encouragement offers he intends soon returning to England, and begs any Gentleman who have occasion for him may apply soon; he will, if desired, wait on any Nobleman or Gentleman at their own Estates.

What sort of problems was this man likely to be called upon to solve and what sort of solutions would he have probably proposed?

3

About 1740 Sir James Hall of Dunglass wrote to the Earl of Marchmont. His spelling was unconventional:

> *No date.* I sent three of my most knowing tennants to Ormistoun where they have learned more of labouring and improveing there grounds in two days then they have doon in all ther life. I have sent for a plewgh that two hors draws as easilie as four ane ordinary plewgh. They when they fallow there grounds to turneip which does ther sheep great advantage and meliorats the grounds as they doe in England. They have all ther grounds inclosed at the tennants charge. His toun is riseing exceedingly, he having 40 kinning lomes and wabsters, and to every 6 lomes has 60 spinsters and all others for cairding, and the wark so that thers not a boy or a girel of 7 years old but has some thing to doe that ye will not see ane in the toun except in ane hour of play. Blacksmiths, shoemakers, candlemakers and baikers, maltsters, etc. make throng doeing. I was twice ther myself and very prittilie interteand, tho the first time J. Cock(burn) happned to be at Edinburgh. Ther is boths building for all thair merchandise and to be market days, and ther is 16 houses contracted for this nixt season. All those are the Great Street, and to be at least two storys high or neare as they please, and in the by lains as they please, but all must be sclated or tiled. What ground he gives them off for a little yeard, they pay for the stance of the house and yeard, as it comes to 22sh. per aiker and 25 years purchase and ane sh. sterling per year. I shall, Dear Marchmont, in a litle time be beter able to let you know more

about it. I have sent for a duble of his tacks and feus. His takes are generaly for 3 lives, and when âne fails he oblidges himself and airs to give another upon the tender of a years rent.

Read this carefully, and then contrast what was going on on Cockburn's estate with what you would expect to find on most estates in Scotland at this period.

4

In 1761 the farming club at Gordon's mill gave the following advice to farmers who were still working the old infield-outfield system:

That every farmer in the summer plough up four acres of his outfield of barren ground (less or more as he can do it well) that he plough it & cross plough it four time and harrow it and gather the stones after each ploughing. This is to be done in the summer when his cattle are idle & his horses have little work. Then he ploughs it again in February or March, and harrows it, by this time it may be well broke. He plants two acres or one half in potatoes in drills with the plough at 4 foot distance betwixt the rows, and a little of his coarsest dung will serve the potatoes. Its not half an acre he has to dung deducting the rows. They are horse-hoed in summer, and kept clean and taken up with the plough in harvest or autumn.

The other two acres, or the other half, to be sown with turnips the beginning of June or end of May. That they be sown in drills of four foot distance, the drills dunged, and the intervals between the drills horse-hoed. He will have good potatoes to feed his family & to sell a part or feed hogs or cows as he pleases. The turnips will save him straw, and feed his cattle, so the very first year he will have a very good return for his labour and no expense.

In the second year its proposed he change the crops & the drills. Plant potatoes where he had his turnips in the former year & sow turnips where his potatoes did grow & horsehoe them as the former year.

The third year if he find his ground in good heart he may sow bear and grass seed, if not he may sow pease, and if he has lime sow a little with them, if not he may sow some ashes, or poultry dung with them, & the fourth cropt to be bear with grass seeds. He will find his land, brought from two shillings or half a crown to be worth from eight to ten shillings an acre, and with proper rest and pasture to be fully as good as his intown.

What difficulties might there be in the way of a tenant farmer who tried to follow this advice?

3 The growth of industry

The linen industry

Apart from agriculture, Scotland's chief industry in the eighteenth century was making linen. This was a complex business, beginning with the growing of flax plants which require a damp, temperate climate and weed-free soil if they are to flourish. When they were mature, the stalks were pulled and dried, and the seeds removed. The stalks were soaked in ponds to rot the outer casing. The flax was then dried and beaten with a wooden knife to remove the last remnants of the outer layers—a process known as 'scutching'. The remaining fibres were then combed out with a 'heckle' or steel-toothed comb, and the flax was ready for spinning. There was hardly any part of the country where no flax was cultivated, but more came from Forfar, Perth and Fife.

It only needed one of the processes either in growing or manufacturing to go wrong and the quality of the finished linen was affected. Much skill and judgment, as well as the right climatic conditions, were therefore needed to produce fine-quality linen. These were frequently lacking, and, in consequence, most of the linen produced in Scotland was coarse. It was also badly bleached. To whiten the brownish linen it had been the custom to soak it in buttermilk and then spread it on bleach-fields, washing it with water scooped out from trenches. It was a process which frequently took more than six months. Nor was the industry well organised. Much linen was produced as a side-line by farmers who sold it at the local market town. There were few large-scale organisations.

As the century wore on, so the industry changed. This was partly due to the activities of the Board of Trustees for

Manufactures, which had been set up by the government in 1727 to increase the efficiency of Scottish industry so that it could compete with foreigners and bring much-needed wealth to the country. It had government money to do this and spent nearly £3000 a year on the linen industry. Some of this went on paying bounties to flax growers and proprietors of bleach-fields, but the board also imported skilled craftsmen from France and Holland in an effort to improve the skill of Scottish operatives. Some progress was made, but German linen still tended to sell cheaper than Scottish cloth, even in British colonies. In 1742, therefore, parliament, partly as a result of pressure from the convention of royal burghs, authorised a bounty to be paid on all linen exported, and in 1746 the British Linen Company was set up to try to improve the organisation of the industry, particularly its marketing overseas. Much of its work involved lending money to business organisations, and in fact it was soon primarily a bank—the ancestor of the British Linen Bank.

The work done by the Linen Company was important because discoveries were being made which needed capital if they were to be properly exploited. In 1728 a scutching machine was invented following a trip to the continent by one of the Board of Trustee's agents. It was adapted for water power, and in 1772 there were two hundred and fifty-two lint mills scutching the flax. By 1817 the number had increased to four hundred—all had needed capital to set them up. Heckling was still done by hand, but it became more and more of a specialist job and heckleries were set up where flax growers brought their crop to be processed. But the most

Value of linen stamped in the country

Year	Value
1758	£ 424 121
1768	599 669
1778	592 023
1788	854 900
1822	1 396 296

important developments took place in bleaching. In 1749 Roebuck had discovered that sulphuric acid could be used in bleaching, and in 1786, following a French invention, James Watt introduced the use of chlorine. Finally, in 1798, Charles Tennant brought chloride of lime into use, and the bleaching industry was on its feet. The plant was expensive and bleach works therefore needed large capital resources. Many such works were set up in Perth, which became the centre of bleaching and dyeing.

While these developments were going on, the quantity of flax grown in Scotland was declining. This was because there was no room for it in the new crop rotations, and other crops could now make just as much money. Attempts to encourage growing large quantities of flax in the Highlands failed, so that to make up the deficit, flax had to be imported. Glasgow and Paisley used foreign yarn to make into fine cloth which sold well. Meanwhile on the east coast flax was brought by sea into Aberdeen to be distributed throughout the North-East to be processed into thread. At first this was then sent south to be woven, but by 1780 most of it was being finished in the town itself. All this needed careful organisation, which was usually in the hands of financiers who bought the flax, put it out to be made up, or perhaps built their own mills to do the job, and then sold the finished cloth at a profit.

Until well after 1800 most of the spinning was still done by women working part-time at home. This was because flax contains a gum which makes the fibres stick together. None of the early spinning machines could cope with this. A wet roller was incorporated into some machines to try to make the flax more slippery, but it was not until 1825 that Kay proved that it could be made workable for spinning machines by steeping it in water for six hours. Within a few years most linen yarn was machine-spun in factories. Weaving was still on hand looms and was a full-time occupation. The hand loom weaver found himself exploited by the financiers. In 1814 a weaver in Forfarshire could expect to clear £1 a week— a very good wage. By the 1820s this had been halved. But worse times were coming, for the power loom was being developed, and this finally put the hand loom weaver out of work completely. By 1820, then, the linen industry was organised and competitive, and the Board of Trustees, no longer needed, was wound up in 1823.

The cotton industry

Meanwhile a competitor had arrived in the shape of cotton. Some cotton thread had been used in weaving in the first half of the eighteenth century, but it was not wholly satisfactory. None the less, imports of cotton increased, especially after 1775 when the American War put a sudden end to the Glasgow tobacco trade. Cotton proved a convenient alternative and imports of raw cotton soared. Processing was no problem. Men and women skilled in making fine linens could easily deal with cotton, which was a much more profitable trade. Vast quantities could be produced by using machines like the 'Jenny' and the water frame, even though neither made really first-rate thread. Water mills were therefore set up housing spinning machines to process the cotton. The first, in 1778, was built at Penicuik. The next at Rothesay, a year later, had 1000 spindles. They were followed by two more at East Kilbride and Glasgow in 1783 and 1784.

A breakthrough came with the invention of Crompton's Mule, which at last spun the thin, strong thread the weavers needed for fine cloth. At first it was a hand-driven machine, unsuitable for factory use. But in 1785 the water frame was modified to spin a better thread and with its help it was possible to process a pound of raw cotton, costing 5s, into thread worth £9 18s 6d. A man with capital, courage and know-how could make money. Richard Arkwright, the English cotton master, had all three, and, impressed by Scotland's

Quantity of raw cotton imported in pounds

1760	96 205
1770	466 589
1780	222 939
1790	2 725 246
1800	4 865 154
1810	9 962 359

N.B. The figure for 1770 was unusually high.

potential of water power, he encouraged David Dale to set up a cotton mill at New Lanark. Dale's career had begun as a linen weaver in Paisley, but latterly he had concentrated on importing yarn and employing weavers to make it up. He now turned to the manufacture of cotton yarn at the New Lanark mills which opened in 1786. They grew in size and importance, but Dale gave less and less of his time to them. In 1787 he had founded two more cotton mills, one at Catrine in Ayrshire and another at Blantyre in partnership with James Montieth. This soon employed more than three hundred and fifty workers, including sixty children who lived in a kind of barracks attached to the factory. A dye works was set up on the same site, but Dale sold this to Montieth's son in 1792. New enterprises beckoned, and he was soon involved in activities as diverse as mining and banking.

In 1797 he sold the New Lanark mills to his future son-in-law, Robert Owen, who made them world-famous by the interest he took in the welfare of his employees. He paid them high wages and

The dreary buildings and tenements of the Lanark cotton mills. When this engraving was done they were still owned by David Dale.

LANARK COTTON MILLS the property of DAVID DALE Esqr

refused to employ any children under the age of ten. The houses he built for his workers were substantial and had good sanitation. He opened company shops where goods were cheaper than average and provided schools for his employees' children. Yet he also made New Lanark pay, even in competition with those employers who exploited their workers shamelessly, forcing them to work long hours for starvation wages, while paying no attention to their living conditions. Owen was thus living proof that high wages and good conditions did not lead to bankruptcy for the firm, and was frequently cited by those who thought that parliament should intervene to control conditions in factories.

Meanwhile other capitalists were setting up cotton mills. Scottish banks were generous in providing credit, which helped would-be merchants and manufacturers. In 1785 John Buchanan, Arkwright's first agent in Scotland, opened a mill at Deanston in Perthshire, and in 1789, encouraged by a local landowner, built another at Ballindalloch in Stirlingshire. His Deanston mill attracted the attention of James Finlay, a Glasgow industrialist, who, like Dale, imported yarn and employed weavers to make it up. He therefore went into partnership with Buchanan, founding the firm of James Finlay & Co. This was soon run almost entirely by James's son, Kirkman Finlay, and became the biggest firm in the trade, taking over the Catrine works from Dale in 1802 and the Ballindalloch works, which Buchanan had sold, in 1808.

Kirkman Finlay's wealth gave him power and prestige, and for many years he was probably the most important man in Glasgow. He became governor of the Forth and Clyde Canal, was eight times president of the Glasgow chamber of commerce, and was made Lord Provost and Dean of Guild. The university made him Dean of Faculty and elected him Rector. Finally, in 1812 he became MP for Glasgow. All this influence he owed to the cloth industry, and most of it to cotton. He was a ruthless salesman, and when Napoleon put an embargo on all British goods Finlay set to work to get round the blockade—with great success. Meanwhile Samuel Crompton, whose invention of the Mule had helped to make it all possible, was living in poverty in England. Business sense counted for more than mechanical ingenuity—not that Finlay's wealth gave him any feeling of security, for he lived in constant fear of revolution and had built up a system of spies so that potential ring-leaders could be arrested and brought to trial.

Other mills, too, were set up. Most were in the West, within easy reach of the port of Glasgow, but there were others, notably in Aberdeen. By 1800 the amount of cotton cloth produced was greater than the production of linen, and there were about forty water-powered spinning mills in the country. Steam power, which by this date was commonly used in England, came later to Scotland. In 1800 there were only eight steam engines in cotton mills in the whole country. This was partly because water power was so plentiful in Scotland, and partly because of the lack of skilled mechanics to service the engines. The same problem applied to the actual spinning machinery, and even in 1824 a mill owner complained that machinery made in Glasgow was inferior to that manufactured in England. Times were, however, changing and by 1830, when there were about a hundred and thirty cotton mills, more than a hundred of them were powered by steam.

The vast increase in production of spun yarn led to great demands on the services of weavers. Though Cartwright had invented a power loom in 1785, it did not really become a commercial proposition until 1807. In the meantime hand loom weavers were paid high wages. They responded by working shorter hours. Years later one of them wrote of those days as 'the daisy portion of weaving', and went on:

> Four days did the weaver work, for then four days was a week as far as working went, and such a week to a skilful weaver brought forty shillings. Sunday, Monday and Tuesday were of course jubilee, lawn frills gorged freely from under the wrists of his fine blue, gilt-buttoned coat. He dusted his head with white flour on Sunday, smirked and wore a cane. Walked in clean slippers on Monday; Tuesday heard him talk war bravado, quote Volney[1] and get drunk. Weaving commenced gradually on Wednesday.

[1] The Comte de Volney was a French political writer whose best-known book, *The Ruins of Empire*, was translated into English and circulated widely in cheap editions. In it the workers are seen as the most important class in the state. The aristocrats and the clergy are mere parasites.

It was too good to last. Hand loom weaving seemed the easy way to make a comfortable living, avoiding the discipline and degradation of factory life. It was therefore taken up by many of those who flocked to the towns to take advantage of the cotton boom. As the

Kirkman Finlay, the Glasgow politician and cotton master.

number of weavers rose, so the rates of pay fell, and the position deteriorated as the number of power looms increased. By 1840 the weavers were earning as little as 7s 6d a week for first-class work. It was no wonder that Kirkman Finlay, who was among the first to introduce the machines, feared that the weavers would rebel and urged the manager of his Catrine works to have cavalry and artillery at hand. In 1816, in the trade depression which followed the end of the war, there was indeed some plotting among the weavers which helped to spark off the State Trials of 1817, but it did no good. Although there was some specialist work that power looms could not do, like the making of fine shawls in which Paisley specialised, their numbers continued to grow, so that by 1820 there were 2000 of them and by 1829, 10 000.

Thus the cotton industry was mechanised and the production of cotton cloth increased by leaps and bounds. This in its turn led to new dye works being set up. Pre-eminent in this field was George MacIntosh who in 1777 extracted a dye from lichen, and then in 1785, with the help of a French expert and capital supplied by Dale, set up a works near Dalmarnock which specialised in turkey-red dyeing. His processes were later copied by others. Meanwhile calico printing was also introduced, being pioneered by the Stirling family who moved their works to the Vale of Leven in 1770. In 1783 Bell invented cylinder printing, which speeded up the process, and as the power looms were introduced and produced larger and larger quantities of rough calico, so the printing works got more and more work.

Vast quantities of raw cotton had to be imported to keep the industry going. To begin with most of it came from the West Indies, for the short staple cotton grown in the USA was difficult to process. But in 1793 the invention of the saw-tooth gin by Whitney overcame this disadvantage and by 1820 more than two-thirds of the cotton was coming from North America. Meanwhile, a large part of the cloth was exported. Some was sent to India, but most went to Germany, Italy, France and Switzerland. At first there was little competition. Napoleon's blockade cut trade with Europe and led to the collapse of many of Glasgow's banks in 1812. With the end of the war in 1815 the continental countries began to establish their own works. By 1830 they all had their own cotton industry, and Scotland was having to fight an uphill battle to maintain her position as a leading cotton exporter. The 'daisy portion' of the cotton industry in Scotland was coming to an end.

The iron industry

Fortunately heavier industries had been growing up to fill the gap. They were based on developments in the iron and coal industry. The first half of the eighteenth century was a period of crisis in the English iron industry, for supplies of timber for charcoal were running out, and the use of coal or coke was only in an experimental stage. Several firms therefore set up furnaces in Scotland to exploit as yet untouched woodlands. The majority of the firms which came from England had only a short life, but Richard Ford & Co. of Lancaster built a furnace at Bunawe in Argyllshire in 1753 which lasted more than a hundred years. Another, established near Inveraray in 1775, lasted until 1813. There was already the Smithfield works in Glasgow, founded in 1734, which provided a large range of wrought iron goods which were sold to the colonies. It was, however, the Seven Years' War which led to the start of large-scale iron production in Scotland. This war cut off supplies of iron from Sweden and Russia, while at the same time increasing demand for munitions. This led to a great expansion of the iron industry and in 1759 the Carron iron works was founded —the first works in Scotland to use coke to smelt iron.

The capital for the works came from three men: Samuel

The Carronade was a very reliable and strongly made weapon. The Carron Company still make them, but only for ornamental use.

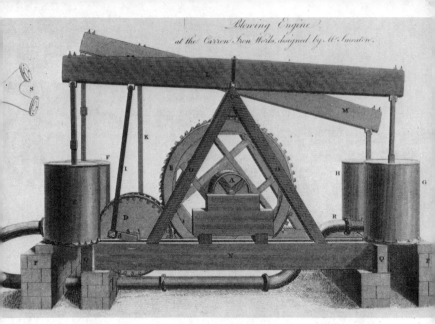

Engine designed by Smeaton to provide the blast for the furnaces at the Carron iron works.

Garbett who was a Birmingham merchant, John Roebuck, a manufacturing chemist from Prestonpans, and William Cadell, a merchant from Cockenzie. The site was carefully chosen. There was water for power and iron ore and coal nearby. The partners first intended to produce rod iron to make into nails, but decided it was more profitable to make cannons instead. At first they had little success, for they lacked skilled workers and the gun barrels kept failing the proof tests. Expert gunfounders were brought in from Sussex, and skilled foundry workers from John Wilkinson's works in Staffordshire. The works were extended, and a steam pumping engine had to be installed to pump water up into reservoirs. A constant supply of water was needed to work the wheels which blew the furnaces. Gradually the guns improved, but not quickly enough to prevent financial crises and the company had to be reorganised in 1771. It was saved by producing more domestic items, such as pots, stoves, grates and spades, by the outbreak of war with the American colonies in 1775 and, above all, by the invention of a new large-calibre naval gun which went into production in 1778. It was called

the Carronade, was sold in large numbers and made the firm a lot of money.

Meanwhile, two discoveries led to further changes in the industry. James Watt, who worked as a technician at Glasgow University, had improved Newcomen's steam pumping engine which worked by atmospheric pressure. Soon he had an engine which worked by steam power, but nobody in Scotland could bore an accurate enough cylinder to make it work properly. He therefore went to Birmingham where, in partnership with Matthew Boulton and with the help of the expertise of John Wilkinson who had invented a machine for boring cannon barrels, he was able to continue his work. His early products were all beam engines and could only be used for pumping, but he developed them rapidly so that by 1781 he had an engine which could drive a wheel. There

This nineteenth-century print shows the Muirkirk iron works. The furnaces are numbered 1 to 4. The forges are in the building marked 5. No. 6 is a rolling mill, 7 the ironstone kiln, 8 the coking ovens and 9 a canal. The workers' houses are on the right.

was no longer any need for iron works to be near water. Then, in 1784, Henry Cort discovered a new and easier method of making wrought iron. The way was clear for a new generation of iron works exploiting these two discoveries.

In fact, since Carron had opened, only one other works had been started in Scotland. This was at Wilsontown in Lanarkshire in 1779. But after 1785 the situation changed radically. In 1786 the Clyde works was set up to make bar iron, and in 1789 the Muirkirk works was founded. In all, between 1785 and 1802, seven new works were opened. After this date there were no more till after 1820, for the market was uncertain. The Carron works did well in wartime selling munitions, but the others found their trade disrupted. They produced such items as agricultural implements, machine parts, water wheels and domestic utensils. They could

47

rely on the Scottish and, to a certain extent, the Irish market but they needed more, and the disruption in trade caused by the war hit them hard. The price of iron fell, and by 1813 many furnaces were out of blast. Conditions improved a little in 1814 but there was another slump after 1815. Even after 1820 trade was slack, for the poor quality of Scottish coal meant that iron was expensive to produce until the discovery of the hot blast in 1828.

The coal industry

The coal industry tended to share the fortunes of iron. In the first half of the eighteenth century most Scottish coal was mined in Midlothian, Fife, Ayrshire and the Glasgow area. The mines were owned by the landowners who either appointed managers to run them or leased them out. The pits were very primitive. They

A section through the colliery workings at Gilmerton showing the miners getting the coal at the faces, and the bearers taking it to the point where it is hoisted to the surface.

consisted of 'drifts' driven into the hillsides along the coal seams or of shallow shafts sunk from the surface into the seam below. Water was a problem. The drifts were commonly drained by digging ditches or tunnels, but the shafts had to be pumped dry. In some cases wind pumps did the work, but water power was more reliable and therefore more widely used. The coal was cut by hewers, who were careful to leave pillars of coal still in place to support the roof. Women bearers took the coal back from the face. Where there was a pit-shaft they sometimes carried their loads up staircases to the surface, though in many cases horse gins provided the lifting power.

Scottish pits were free of fire-damp, so that explosions were rare. None the less the work was hard and dangerous, and it was never easy to get miners. In 1606 the Scottish parliament had passed an act whereby pit-workers were bound for life to the

mine in which they worked. As the years passed this law was rigorously applied and even extended, so that in the eighteenth century it was taken for granted that miners' children had to follow their fathers and work in the pit. Even this failed to solve the labour shortage, and coal owners were forced to offer high pay to their workers. In 1763 Adam Smith reckoned a hewer could earn 2s 6d a day. He had to pay his bearer out of this, but it was double what most labourers could earn and the bearer was usually one of his family. Coupled with high wages were other benefits. Housing, though primitive, was either free or very cheap and many owners provided for their workers in sickness and old age. Yet still the mines were shunned by other workers and the colliers in their isolated communities were looked on as little better than slaves.

Scottish mines were much less advanced than those in Northumberland and Durham, but up until 1760 they produced enough coal for the country's needs—about 500 000 tons a year. This output, conveyed from the pit-head in small carts or else by pack-horses, was consumed in domestic heating, salt-boiling, lime-burning and glass-making. Some, from the Ayrshire pits, was exported to Ireland, but the coastal trade within Scotland was hindered by customs duties.

After 1760, however, there was a dramatic increase in demand, at first due to the new iron works whose furnaces consumed more than seven tons of coal to produce one ton of iron. At the same time demand from the traditional users was increasing and output rose to just over 1 500 000 tons in 1808 and reached about 2 500 000 tons in 1814. This five-fold increase in less than sixty years meant that great changes had to be made in every aspect of mining. A new system of hewing coal was introduced so that all the coal could now be extracted instead of leaving up to a third of it standing as pillars to support the roof. Wooden wagonways were laid down and trucks provided to speed coal on its way from the face, and some large pits even brought horses underground to replace the bearers. Deeper shafts were sunk—as far as four hundred feet in some places. Water-powered pumps were only really effective down to two hundred and fifty feet, so steam pumps had to be used. Ventilation, too, became more of a problem, solved by sinking additional shafts to provide a circulation of air.

The demand for miners increased and the system of 'tied' labour was abolished in stages between 1775 and 1799 to try to attract fresh workers. In addition wages were increased until in 1808 colliers in Alloa could earn 4s 6d a day, which was, it was noted, 'better than the pay of a lieutenant in the army'. Even so, the country remained short of miners until immigrants from Ireland solved the problem.

Existing mines could not cope with the demand and new fields had to be opened up. Transport was the chief difficulty. It could cost up to a shilling a mile to move a ton of coal, an enormous sum when the price of good coal at the pit-head was only about seven shillings a ton. Coal owners were therefore enthusiastic road-makers and laid wooden or even iron wagonways to connect the mine to a convenient port. But it was not until the Lowland canals had been engineered that it was possible to exploit the coal measures to the east of Glasgow to the full.

All these developments demanded skill and money. To begin with the skilled men had to be imported from Northumberland and Durham, but by 1800 Scotsmen like Robert Bald were as good mining engineers as any in Britain. The money, too, had to come from outside the industry. Few landowners could, for instance, afford to buy a steam pumping engine costing £1300 and pay its running costs of about £10 a week, while the rapid opening up of new mines was quite beyond them. Instead the capital came from business men, cotton magnates and iron masters, so that by 1820 the industry was passing out of the hands of the landowners. The pace of change was uneven. The coalfields of the East were generally less go-ahead than those in the West and clung longer to the old ways, but by and large the coal industry was to be able to cope with the huge expansion in demand from the iron industry after 1828.

Summing up

By 1820 Scottish industry had altered profoundly in every way. In the first half of the eighteenth century only the linen industry was of any real economic significance, and that was poorly organised. State help and technical developments, especially in bleaching and dyeing, gave capitalists the chance to make money and the industry prospered. Its competitor, cotton, benefited from the expertise of spinners and weavers who had learned their skills in the linen trade. It was also helped by the fact that it offered high returns to those who put their money into it. Capital was, therefore, freely available to finance the manufacture and sale of cotton. As a result the industry developed rapidly, and helped the cotton masters to wealth and power before competition from the continent made their task more difficult. In the meantime the iron and coal industries had developed to a considerable size from very small beginnings. All this resulted in the concentration of industry and population in the central Lowlands, and labour came from the Highlands and from Ireland to man the machines and swell the growing industrial towns.

The growth of such towns was extraordinarily rapid. For instance, Glasgow's population stood at 32 700 in 1755. By 1821 it had risen to 147 000, while between 1755 and 1801 the number of inhabitants of Paisley rocketed from 6800 to 31 200. The new areas in such towns were neither elegant nor healthy. To accommodate the newcomers cheap tenements were built. Crowded together to save land, they lacked both drains and a supply of drinking water. They frequently had no schools, no churches and were inadequately policed. The lives of their inhabitants revolved round the factories in which they worked.

Some contrived to live quite well. In good times they could afford reasonable food and even good furniture. But there was no security. When trade was bad they might be unemployed and they and their families would go hungry. When there was no work in the mills, some tried making cloth on hand looms in their own homes, but after 1810 this paid worse than factory work even if all the family co-operated and two looms were kept going. Even when trade was booming the long hours of work in unhealthy factories coupled with the cramped living conditions took their toll. Bronchitis and tuberculosis were common complaints among textile workers and many were invalids in their thirties. They then had to rely on their children to keep them. If they, too, became ill, then the outlook was bleak indeed. It is no wonder that the weavers formed trade unions and were sometimes driven

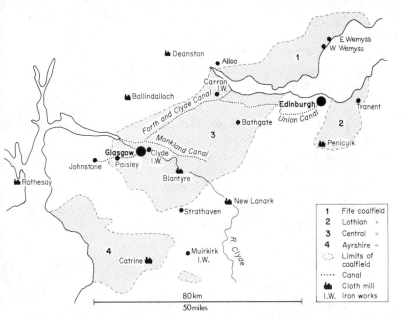

The industrial Lowlands showing canals, iron works and the principal cotton mills.

to violence. They knew all too well what might lie before them—a steady decline, perhaps to end their days in one of the lodging houses in the slums described by J. C. Symons in a report to parliament in 1839:

'The wynds', he wrote, 'consist of long lanes so narrow that a cart could with difficulty pass along them; out of these open the "closes", which are courts about 15 to 20 feet square, round which the houses, mostly of three stories high are built; the centre of the court is the dung-hill . . . The houses are for the most part let in flats, either to the lowest class of labourers or prostitutes or to lodging-keepers; . . . these latter places are the resting place of outcasts of every grade of wretchedness and destitution. In the more costly of these abodes, where separate beds are furnished at the price of 3d per night, the thieves and prostitutes chiefly congregate. . . . I did not believe until I visited the wynds of Glasgow, that so large an amount of filth, crime, misery and disease existed on one spot in any civilised country.'

Documents

1

The following evidence was given by Mr. Archibald Buchanan, a partner in James Finlay & Co., to a parliamentary committee which was enquiring into conditions in textile mills in 1816:

At the Catrine works there are 875 persons employed, of whom 22 males and 37 females are under ten years of age. I suppose the youngest may be 8 or 9; we have no wish to employ them under ten years of age.

What are your hours of work?—Our working hours are twelve hours in the day. They begin at 6 o'clock in the morning, they stop at half-past seven at night, and they are allowed half an hour to breakfast, and an hour to dinner.

You have not observed that the twelve hours work has interfered with the health of the children?—I have not . . . I have seen many instances of children that were taken in the works as young as six, whose health did not appear at all to suffer; on the contrary, when they got to greater maturity, they appeared as healthy stout people as any in the country . . . They go to all trades, masons and joiners, and weavers, and so on.

Are they as tall?—Yes, I do not see any difference.

Do you conceive that the habits of regularity they are taught in the works, are advantageous to them in their pursuits afterwards?—I should think it was; that is the chief advantage tradesmen think they have in employing children from the factories.

That is, from their habits of industry?—Yes, and the ingenuity they acquire in the works.

Are the parents generally very desirous to send their children to you, or not?—Very desirous.

What are the weekly wages a child of nine years old will acquire in your works?—The children of 9 years are generally learners, and receive 1s 6d to 2s per week, according to their ability.

2

Robert Owen also gave evidence to the same committee:

Seventeen years ago, a number of individuals, with myself, purchased the New Lanark establishment from the late Mr. Dale, of Glasgow. At that period I find that there were 500 children, who had been taken from poor-houses, chiefly in Edinburgh, and those children were generally from the age of five and six, to seven and eight; they were so taken because Mr. Dale could not, I learned afterwards, obtain them at a more advanced period of life; if he did not take them at those ages, he could not obtain them at all. The hours of work at that time were thirteen, inclusive of meal times, and an hour and a half was allowed for meals. I very soon discovered that although those children were very well fed, well clothed, well lodged, and very great care taken of them when out of the mills, their growth and their minds were materially injured by being employed at those ages within the cotton mills for eleven hours and a half per day. It is true that those children, in consequence of being so well fed and clothed and lodged, looked fresh, and to a superficial observer, healthy in their coun-tenances; yet their limbs were generally deformed, their growth was stunted, and although one of the best school-masters upon the old plan was engaged to instruct those children regularly every night, in general they made but a very slow progress, even in learning the common alphabet . . .

a What, according to Mr. Buchanan, were the advantages of a few years factory work for young children?

b What advantages did the factory owner reap from employing them?

c On what points did Mr. Buchanan and Mr. Owen contradict each other?

d Which report do you find the more convincing? Why?

3

The following notes were made by Mr. R. H. Franks, a parliamentary inspector, who interviewed many mineworkers in the east of Scotland in 1842:

No. 1. Janet Cumming, 11 years old, bears coals:

Works with father; has done so for two years. Father gangs at two in the morning; I gang with the women at five, and come up at five at night; work all night on Fridays, and come away at twelve in the day.

I carry the large bits of coal from the wall-face to the pit bottom, and the small pieces called chows in a creel; the weight is usually a hundredweight; does not know how many pounds there are in the hundredweight, but it is some work to carry; it takes three journeys to fill a tub of 4 cwt. The distance varies, as the work is not always on the same wall; sometimes 150 fathom, whiles 250. The roof is very low; I have to bend my back and legs, and the water comes frequently up to the calves of my legs; has no likening for the work; father makes me like it; mother did carry coal, she is not needed now, as sisters and brothers work on father and uncle's account. Never got hurt, but often obliged to scramble out when bad air was in the pit.

Father lately got crushed by a big coal falling, and was by for seven weeks; was supported by William Bennet's and John Craig's societies, to which he subscribed; believes he got 8s weekly from the two.

I am learning to read at the night school; am in the twopenny book; sometimes to Sabbath-school. Jesus was God; David wrote the Bible; has a slight knowledge of the first six questions in the shorter catechism.

a What were the chief dangers of working in the pit?

b Assuming that conditions did not alter, what do you think the future held for Janet Cumming?

c What job in the pit was done by the men?

4 Communications and trade

Improvements in agriculture and the development of industry meant that communications had to be improved. Farmers needed to shift tons of lime on to their land, and to get their produce to towns to market in greater quantities than before. Cloth merchants had to be able to rely on getting the raw material to the factories and the finished goods away quickly and cheaply. The iron works consumed huge quantities of ore and coal while producing an ever-increasing flow of heavy and unmanageable goods ranging from kettles to cannons, all of which had to be carted away and sold at a competitive price. In the middle of the eighteenth century it was clear that the roads could not cope with this burden of heavy, bulky goods. Most of Scotland's rivers are too shallow and fast-flowing to be suitable for traffic. Wagonways were in their infancy. Canals seemed the only answer.

Canals

Making a canal was a very difficult business. The route had to be carefully surveyed, for the canal bed must be dead level. Slopes had to be negotiated by locks, which are both expensive and time-wasting, so that the shortest route was often not the best. Once the line of the canal was decided, then the land had to be bought. There was usually little difficulty about this in the eighteenth century, for a canal running through your land tended to increase the value of the estate. When the canal was made it had to be lined with clay to make it waterproof, and the banks made secure from the wash of barges, while the locks had to be lined with masonry. Finally, of course, it had to have a supply of water to keep it full. Frequently reservoirs had to be specially constructed for this purpose. Clearly, all this was very expensive, and before a canal was begun it had to be authorised by an act of parliament which allowed the proprietors to borrow money up to a certain sum from the public. Interest was to be paid out of the tolls which were charged to canal users.

The Forth–Clyde Canal

The first canal of consequence in Scotland was the Forth–Clyde Canal, which was intended to provide an easy east–west trade route. Proposals to link the two rivers had been made in the seventeenth century, but real progress was not made until 1763, when John Smeaton was commissioned by the Board of Trustees for Manufactures to make a detailed survey. He proposed a canal from the river Carron to Yoker Burn, five feet deep, twenty-seven miles long, costing £78 970. This scheme enraged the Glasgow merchants who had taken it for granted that the canal would terminate in Glasgow itself. They therefore commissioned other surveys, by James Watt and Robert Mackell, for a small canal to serve Glasgow itself. Such pretensions excited scorn in Edinburgh, one of whose citizens described the Glasgow scheme as 'a ditch, a gutter, a mere puddle'. Tempers ran high but the Glasgow merchants got little support outside their own city. In 1767 Smeaton made another survey, this time working on the basis of a canal seven feet deep, to cater for sea-going vessels and with a cut through to Glasgow. The total cost was estimated at £147 337, but he warned that 'there must be a degree of latitude in an affair of such great consequence'. His report was accepted, and, backed by a number of noblemen and merchants, the necessary act was passed by parliament in 1768. This authorised the proprietors to borrow money up to £150 000 immediately, and to raise a further £50 000 if necessary. A little later Smeaton was appointed head engineer—a position which carried a salary of £500 a year. Robert Mackell was appointed sub-engineer, and was paid £315 a year.

All now seemed set. Those Glasgow merchants who still

pressed for their so-called 'small' canal were bought off with a grant of £1500 to cover the costs of their survey. The Carron Company, which wanted large-scale engineering works to be undertaken to improve access to its works, was ignored. This led to accusations that the line of the canal had been deliberately laid down to benefit Sir Lawrence Dundas across whose estate it ran. Such charges were indignantly denied and the work went ahead employing more than 1000 men. In June 1770 the line at the western end was changed so that it now joined the Clyde at Bowling. This saved money and took the main canal nearer to Glasgow. In 1773 an agreement was reached with the Carron Company for the construction of a branch to link with their works. By 1775 there was water in a large part of the canal, but money ran out and it became clear that at least £100 000 more would be needed to finish the canal. The extra money. was raised, and the work continued. The waterway was opened in stages, but it was not complete until 1790. In all, including the cuts to Carron and Glasgow, it was thirty-nine miles long and had thirty-nine locks. It had cost more than £300 000 and had taken more than twenty years to make.

It brought considerable benefits, particularly after a branch was opened in 1791 which linked it to the Monkland Canal. This led to the growth of the town of Port Dundas (now a part of Glasgow), which relied entirely on the canal for its livelihood. The main traffic consisted of coal barges. In 1800 24 500 tons of coal were carried. By 1808 this figure had increased to 80 500 tons. Herring boats sometimes used the canal to cut through from coast to coast, and a thriving passenger trade built up after the provision of special passenger boats in 1809. Experiments were made with new types of boat. In 1803 a steam-driven craft—the 'Charlotte Dundas'—was tried out but was abandoned because it was feared the wash from her paddles would damage the banks. In 1819 a cast-iron barge went into service. Meanwhile, the canal also made money. The first dividend was not paid until 1800 and amounted to 10%, but by 1817 it had risen to 25% and remained at this level for some years. Thus the shareholders were happy, the manufacturers found their transport costs lower, and the consumer enjoyed lower prices.

The Monkland Canal

Similar blessings were brought by the Monkland Canal, which ran from Glasgow to Woodhall. Its aim was to open up the coalfields to the east of the city. It was surveyed by James Watt in 1769, and the necessary act was passed in 1770 authorising the proprietors to raise £15 000. The canal was not finished until 1793, by which time it was twelve miles long and had cost £120 000. But it proved a profitable waterway as the coal and iron industries developed in Lanarkshire, and branches were built. There were early difficulties in getting an adequate supply of water, but these were overcome, and in 1817 the dividend paid was equivalent to £72 on each original £100 share. The main proprietors were Andrew Stirling, a coal owner, and William and George Stirling, partners in a firm of Glasgow merchants.

The Union Canal

The Monkland Canal assured a supply of cheap coal for Glasgow. A similar service was to be provided for Edinburgh by the Edinburgh and Glasgow Union Canal. Most of Edinburgh's coal in 1790 came from Alloa, Wemyss or even Newcastle, and was subject to a duty of 3s 6d a ton. It was hoped that by navigating a canal from Edinburgh to a convenient point on the Forth and Clyde Canal, the coal from the Monkland fields would become cheaply available in the capital. Discussion of the scheme certainly began as early as 1791, and by 1798 no fewer than five possible lines had been surveyed. None of them was easy and estimates of cost were about £250 000. It was difficult to choose between the various schemes; it was wartime and money was tight. The whole idea was therefore shelved until 1813 when the high price of coal re-awakened interest. A new survey was made by Hugh Baird, who had been an engineer on the Forth and Clyde Canal. He suggested a branch from the Forth and Clyde at Falkirk to a basin at Fountainbridge in Edinburgh. This raised a great storm because it had been taken for granted that the canal would terminate in the port of Leith. The Edinburgh shippers therefore complained. Those whose land was by-passed by Baird's scheme protested that it was a stupid route to follow, and produced con-

Slateford aqueduct, which carries the Union Canal over the Water of Leith, was designed by Hugh Baird, though Telford's advice was also taken.

vincing reasons. Those whose land would be on the new route, on the other hand, pointed out its obvious advantages, which ought, they contended, to be clear to all right-thinking people. And so the arguments continued, with many supporting a scheme originally proposed by Rennie in 1798, which took a quite different route.

Such disagreements meant unnecessary delay and expense. In 1815 Telford was called in and declared in favour of Baird's plan, but when the bill authorising it came before the Lords it was defeated. Rennie's scheme for a canal from Leith to Broomielaw was now brought forward, but few were prepared to back it and in 1816 all eventually agreed to support Baird's scheme. Its cost was estimated at £264 910. The necessary bill was passed in 1817. Baird's salary was fixed at £500 a year, provided the work was completed within five years and cost no more than £240 500. Work began in March 1818, and was completed on time in 1823. But the cost was much greater than anticipated—more than £450 000 for a canal thirty-one miles long, with only eleven locks.

There was some excuse for over-spending. The original line had been altered in several places to please local landowners and land had sometimes proved more expensive than anticipated. The canal was, moreover, a much more original and complicated piece of civil engineering than its predecessors, having three aqueducts, all longer than those on any other Scottish canal, and a tunnel nearly seven hundred yards long—unique in Scotland. At any rate, whatever the cause, the canal started business with a large burden of debt.

Fortunately traffic was such that this burden could be reduced. Goods traffic was mostly into Edinburgh, the main cargoes being coal, timber, stone, slate, brick, sand and lime. Passengers, on the other hand, provided a two-way traffic. By 1835 more than 120 000 a year were being carried. In spite of growing competition from coaches, the horse-drawn passenger boats, which took fourteen hours to do the journey from Edinburgh to Glasgow, made a clear profit of £3000 in 1839. They travelled so fast that the public were warned that it was dangerous to walk along the tow-path. They helped the canal to pay its way, and it was not until the opening of the Edinburgh and Glasgow Railway that it once more got into serious financial difficulties. But that is another story.

The Paisley and Johnstone Canal

Another Lowland canal had a less fortunate history than the Union. This was the one proposed by the Earl of Eglinton to run from Glasgow through to the Ayrshire coast at Ardrossan. The canal was expected to give rise to a new port in the Ardrossan area, and to carry a vast mineral and goods traffic as well as many passengers. The route and proposed harbour were surveyed by Rennie and John Ainslie and the cost in 1804 was estimated at £130 960. In 1805 Telford suggested a slight alteration in the route which would avoid the locks between Glasgow and Johnstone. This raised the cost to £134 500, with annual revenue estimated at £13 699. There was great enthusiasm, particularly among those whose land stood to gain in value. The necessary act was passed in 1806, and soon more than £115 000 had been raised. Work on the canal began in 1807 and the section between Paisley and Johnstone was opened in 1810. In 1811 the canal was open right from Glasgow to Johnstone. It was an excellent waterway, with an aqueduct, two short tunnels and no locks to delay traffic. But, as usual, it had proved much more expensive than anticipated and there was no money left to continue the canal to the coast. This, it was estimated, would cost £143 500. Nobody was prepared to advance the necessary money. In 1817 the Earl of Eglinton asked the Prime Minister for a government loan of £135 000, but was refused on the grounds that a new port at Ardrossan was unnecessary as the Clyde had recently been deepened to take ocean-going vessels. The last chance of completing the canal was gone.

One of the main reasons for the difficulty in raising money from the public was that the canal proprietors were already deeply in debt, and the revenue from traffic was not enough to cover running expenses, let alone pay off the debt. The situation was improved by fixing rates for goods which competed with those charged by carters, and by expanding passenger traffic. Even so, the debts of the canal were not paid off until it was taken over by the Glasgow and South Western Railway Company in 1869.

So much for the canals of the industrial Lowlands. All were the result of bold and imaginative schemes and depended on heavy industry for their traffic. All presented difficult engineering problems and cost far more than was anticipated. Few of the proprietors who subscribed to these canals made anything worth while from the dividends they received. Often, however, they gained in other ways. Sometimes a coalfield which they owned was opened up, or perhaps the lime necessary to sweeten the land on their estates could now be brought in more cheaply. In the long run they rarely lost. The country certainly gained, for the canals lowered transport costs and encouraged the development of heavy industries in areas which had the necessary mineral resources but which had been inaccessible hitherto.

The Aberdeenshire Canal

Three more canals deserve mention. Two of them were intended to shorten sea-routes. The third was the only canal made in a predominantly agricultural area—the Aberdeenshire Canal, which ran from Aberdeen to Inverurie. It was planned in 1793, and its aim was to encourage the growth of new industries in the Inverurie area, as well as providing a convenient outlet for the increasing crop yield of that part of Aberdeenshire. By 1795 £11 000 had been subscribed, and in 1796 the necessary act of parliament was passed authorising the raising of £20 000. In fact only £17 700 had been subscribed when, in 1797, Rennie was appointed chief engineer. Work on the canal was under way in 1798 but money ran out in 1799. A further act of parliament had to be passed in 1801 to allow more money to be raised, and by the time the eighteen-mile canal was opened in 1805, it had cost £44 000. Even so, the work had been skimped. It was only twenty feet wide instead of twenty-seven, and three feet six inches deep instead of four feet. What was more, the year after it was opened some of the seventeen locks collapsed, and the canal had to be closed while they were repaired. At best, the canal was only open to traffic from April to December. It carried grain, meal, slate and stone down to Aberdeen, and lime, coal, dung, bark and bones up to Inverurie, as well as a fairly flourishing two-way passenger traffic. For many years it was in very severe financial difficulties, but by the 1840s, when it was replaced by a railway, it was beginning to make money. Meanwhile Inverurie and Kintore had both grown in size, and land near the canal had increased in value.

The Crinan Canal

By the time the Aberdeenshire Canal was opened in 1805, work had been more or less completed on another, and much more difficult venture—the Crinan Canal. The purpose of this was to provide a waterway across the Mull of Kintyre, and thus shorten the sea journey from Glasgow to the North-West by about seventy-five miles, including the awkward passage round the Mull of Kintyre. The idea had long been current, but it was not until 1771 that the Glasgow magistrates petitioned the commissioners for the forfeited estates to use some of their funds to get the project off the ground. James Watt did a survey of two possible routes, but no further action was taken until 1792 when John Rennie made another survey, estimating the cost of a canal twelve feet deep from Ardrishaig to Crinan at about £63 000. In the end the proprietors decided that the canal ought to be fifteen feet deep

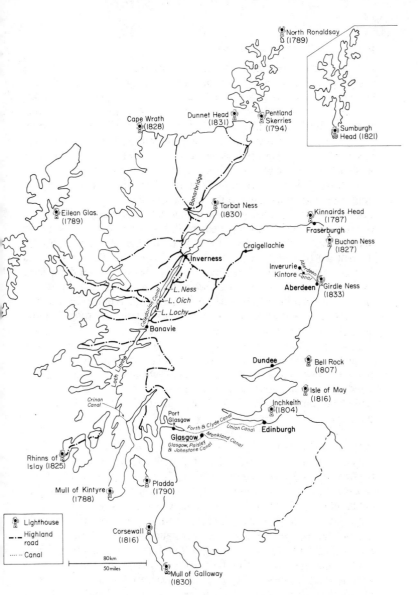

North Ronaldsay
(1789)

Sumburgh
Head (1821)

Cape Wrath
(1828)

Dunnet Head
(1831)

Pentland
Skerries
(1794)

Eilean Glas.
(1789)

Tarbat Ness
(1830)

Kinnairds Head
(1787)

Fraserburgh

Buchan Ness
(1827)

Craigellachie

Inverness

Inverurie
Kintore

Aberdeen Canal

Aberdeen

Girdle Ness
(1833)

L. Ness
L. Oich
L. Lochy

Caledonian Canal

Bonarbridge

Banavie

Loch Linnhe

Dundee

Bell Rock
(1807)

Isle of May
(1816)

Inchkeith
(1804)

Crinan Canal

Port
Glasgow

Forth & Clyde Canal

Union Canal

Glasgow

Monkland Canal

Edinburgh

Glasgow, Paisley
& Johnstone Canal

Rhinns of
Islay (1825)

Pladda
(1790)

Mull of Kintyre
(1788)

Corsewall
(1816)

Mull of Galloway
(1830)

Lighthouse

Highland
road

Canal

80km
50 miles

Canals, roads and lighthouses.

65

to take larger vessels. This increased the estimated cost to £107 700. The necessary act of parliament was passed in 1793, and enough money was promised for work to begin.

Progress was slow. The works were in a remote area, and difficult to keep supplied with provisions and with building stone. Skilled workmen were almost unobtainable and the terrain, too, was very rough. The whinstone through which a way had to be blasted was unusually hard and the marshland, in places, almost impassable. Money was always short. Most had been promised from England and it was often difficult to get the shareholders to meet their obligations. With the help of a government loan of £25 000 the canal was opened in 1802—though only for boats drawing less than eight feet. In 1804 it was still unfinished and the government made another loan of £25 000. By 1813 numerous defects had appeared. The water supply was insufficient, the lock gates were rotting, projections of rock were constantly damaging boats, and after heavy rain the bank was liable to burst. Parliament was asked for yet another loan and Telford was sent to survey the canal to see what was needed. He found that though £184 000 had already been spent a further £18 000 was necessary. Once again the government footed the bill, but this time put the canal under the control of the commissioners who were in charge of the work on the Caledonian Canal. Under their superintendence the canal was put into order, though it has always been difficult and expensive to maintain.

The Caledonian Canal

But the maintenance of the Crinan Canal was the least of the commissioners' worries. Their chief task was the making of the Caledonian Canal, a waterway linking Loch Linnhe to the Moray Firth, cutting Scotland in two and providing an easy east–west route, avoiding the stormy journey round Cape Wrath. The idea had been considered as early as 1726, and James Watt had made a survey for the commissioners of the forfeited estates in 1773, estimating the cost at £164 032. Action was finally taken in 1803 after a further survey by Telford, who put the cost of a canal twenty feet deep at £350 000. The scheme was enthusiastically supported by shipowners in the major ports, and by the government who believed the canal would attract employment to the Highlands and thus cut emigration. In addition, it would safeguard shipping from French privateers. Parliament accordingly gave their blessing, granted £20 000 to the project and appointed five commissioners to manage the works. Telford was the chief engineer.

The difficulties were formidable. The canal had to link Loch Linnhe to Loch Lochy, a distance of about seven miles, and Loch Lochy to Loch Oich, about two miles. Much dredging was necessary to deepen Loch Oich, and a further stretch of four miles separated it from Loch Ness. Finally, from Loch Ness to the Moray Firth was eight miles. The levels were different and in all twenty-nine locks were needed. The canal took more than twenty years to build and cost nearly £1 000 000, most of which was provided by the government. The project caught the imagination of many writers who came to admire the works. It seemed that resources had been gathered from all over the United Kingdom to make the canal a success. Steam pumping engines built by Boulton and Watt in Birmingham kept the great sea locks clear of water while work was in progress. Welsh oak was used for some of the lock gates, with Derbyshire iron for the fittings. But most of the work was done by Highlanders who were unused to navvying. Workmen tended to drift away at harvest time, or when the herring shoals were off the coast. Once a gang was driven from Loch Oich by the local landowner, Macdonell of Glengarry, who claimed they would spoil his fishing. When at work the men were liable to drink too much whisky so the commissioners set up a brewery to supply them with beer instead. It was often difficult to get provisions and the Bank of Scotland at Inverness was frequently hard put to provide enough cash to pay the workers. The terrain was very rough and the climate hard. Sometimes the work was inadequately supervised and was shoddily done with inferior materials. Thus in 1837 the masonry of the locks at Banavie was described as 'execrable', so bad that the inspecting engineer thought the contractor must have believed the canal would never be opened 'and that his locks would consequently never require to come into actual operation'. None the less, when the canal was first opened in 1822, still unfinished, it was hailed as an engineering masterpiece.

In fact its impact, and that of the Crinan Canal, was disappointing. Almost before they were finished they were outdated by the development of steam boats. These made the passages round the Mull of Kintyre and through the Pentland Firth safer and quicker than before, as did the work of the commissioners of northern lighthouses. The delays at the canal locks were such that it was soon as quick to go round the Mull as through the Crinan. Moreover, boats were getting bigger so that neither canal could take them. Thus their traffic was limited to coasters and fishing vessels. In the early years even sailing ships hesitated to use the Caledonian Canal, for there was no tow-path through the lochs and the ship masters were nervous of sailing along these narrow waters as they had not enough room to cope with sudden gusts of wind which might drive them on to the bank. In any case they might be held up by contrary winds. Steam tugs provided the answer, but it was a long time before the commissioners would allow them. Meanwhile the canal did not bring the expected industry and employment to the area and emigration continued apace.

Yet for all that, people were right to feel proud of the Caledonian Canal. It was a great investment of talent and wealth, made by a nation which until 1815 was at war and then had to cope with a great economic crisis. It was a gesture of confidence. Only an optimistic society would have made it. What was more, it represented a triumph of technology over formidable obstacles. The same was no doubt true of other canals, but the idea of linking two wild northern oceans through a barren and—to most people— barbarous glen captured the imagination in somewhat the same way as space travel does today. It was also of much more immediate practical use. Canals were, it is true, outdated by railways or by fast steam boats. But the making of the railways would have been much more difficult without the lessons learned in engineering canals, and the first steam boat, the 'Charlotte Dundas', was, after all, designed for use on the Forth–Clyde Canal.

Lowland roads

Though canals could carry heavy loads cheaply, they could not by themselves provide a complete transport system. An efficient

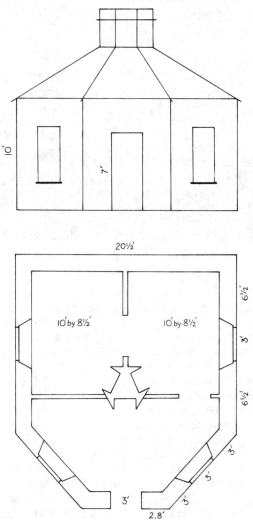

This plan and elevation are copied from the working drawings used by the builder of this toll house on the Fochabers road in 1809. The total cost of building was £126 5s 4d.

Smeaton's bridge over the Tay at Perth.

system of roads was needed as well. At the beginning of the eighteenth century this was conspicuously lacking. Before 1750 English roads were poor: Scotland's were almost non-existent. Tracks existed, and most of the traffic on them consisted of pack-horses which carried about two hundredweight each at a walking pace. Wheeled traffic was almost unknown and hopelessly impracticable. When Lord Lovat decided to travel from Inverness to Edinburgh by coach in 1742 the journey—about a hundred and sixty miles—took him eleven days. The rear axle broke twice and the front axle once, shattered by the rock-strewn, water-scarred surfaces. Only in or near towns were the roads properly made, and in the winter communications might break down completely for days—or even weeks—at a time. There were few bridges and the fords and ferries could be dangerous on Scotland's swift flowing rivers. Thus there was every incentive to stay at home, and since not many people travelled, inns were few and poor.

Attempts were made to keep roads in repair and even improve them. By an act of 1669 all able-bodied men could be called on to work six days a year on the roads. In addition landowners could be required to pay an assessment of up to 10s a year for every £100 Scots their lands were valued for rent. In practice the statute work was in many cases completely ignored. Sometimes men turned out for a couple of days or paid a small sum of money instead. Perhaps a few ruts and potholes would be filled in or a ditch cleared, but after the first rain all would be as bad again. Clearly something more systematic was required. Turnpike trusts seemed to be the answer. The theory behind such trusts was simple. An act of parliament authorised some of the local gentry to raise money to make and maintain roads at their own expense, on the understanding that they would charge tolls to the road-users. These tolls were to be used to maintain the road and to pay interest to those whose money had been used in making it. The making and maintaining of the road was in the hands of con-tractors appointed by the trustees, and supervised by a surveyor whom they appointed. Usually the trustees were the owners of the land through which the road ran. Even if the traffic on the road did not bring in enough to pay interest on their money they did not mind, for the turnpike made their estates more accessible and increased the value of the land. But some trusts found their tolls did not bring in enough even to maintain the road. In such cases the tolls were increased or extra gates were put in. Even so, some turnpike roads never paid and were badly maintained.

None the less, the turnpike system gradually improved Scottish roads, beginning in 1714 when the first turnpike act for Scotland was passed. It applied to roads in Midlothian. The next was passed in 1751, and by 1844 three hundred and fifty acts had been passed setting up trusts all over the country. Slowly communications improved. In 1749 a coach service was begun between Glasgow and Edinburgh. The forty-six-mile journey took twelve hours. By 1799 the time had been reduced to six hours. The service between Edinburgh and London ran twice a day instead of once a month, and took sixty hours instead of a fortnight. In 1788 a direct coach service was opened between London and Glasgow, and as the towns of Scotland were linked by turnpikes so coach services were introduced to take advantage of them. Bridges, too, were built; the finest, over the Tay at Perth, was designed by Smeaton. It cost £26 000, half of it from public subscription, and was completed in 1771. By 1800 the network of main roads over the Lowlands was more or less complete, and attention could be devoted to less important routes. Most main roads today follow the track of the turnpikes, and the gatehouses often survive.

Highland roads

So much for the Lowlands. The Highlands were a different matter, for here the movement of traffic was not sufficient to make turn-pike roads over such difficult country an economic proposition. True, there were some roads and bridges which had been financed by the government and built by soldiers organised by General Wade and Edward Caulfield between 1725 and 1770. But these were military roads, designed for moving troops to strategically important areas. They were often steep and were not designed to carry heavy traffic. Nor had they been well maintained. By the end of the eighteenth century much of the eight hundred miles of mili-tary roads in the Highlands was almost unusable and many of the bridges were ruinous. In any case the economic needs of the area had not been considered when the roads were made: the necessity to improve the road south for the cattle drovers and fish sellers, and by every means to try to stop emigration.

In 1800 the problem was a major government consideration and they decided to take a hand in Highland road building. They offered to pay half the cost of any Highland road construction approved by their commissioners, provided that the local land-owners found the rest. The construction of the road was to be undertaken by contractors, supervised by a team of surveyors, headed by Telford. The landowners jumped at the chance of making roads on the cheap and readily came forward with sug-gested routes, all of which were carefully surveyed by Telford or one of his team. If the suggestion was approved, then tenders were invited from contractors to make the road according to the specification laid down by the surveyors. Once all the tenders were in, the commissioners and the landowners had to decide which to accept. This could be difficult. The government surveyors were experienced men, and usually knew quite well how much a road ought to cost—though even they sometimes made mistakes. The

An engraving of Telford's bridge at Craigellachie. It was replaced by a steel structure of the same design which has now been by-passed by a box-girder bridge.

contractors, on the other hand, were often totally inexperienced, and in their anxiety to get the contract offered to do the job at much too low a price. The landowners were commonly anxious to accept the lowest figure, but the commissioners knew that this meant that the work would be skimped, or the contractor would go bankrupt—or perhaps both. They therefore tried to appoint reliable men who made realistic tenders. Sometimes they got their way. Sometimes they did not, the contractor ran out of money, and the work had to be completed by his backers. There were two of these, and before a contract was awarded they had to guarantee to finance the completion of the road if the contractor went bankrupt. All this meant trouble and delay.

One thing was clear. However low the price, the quality of the road must not be allowed to suffer. 'We should deem ourselves to be bad stewards of public expenditure,' wrote the commissioners, 'did we not labour for posterity as well as for the present generation.' Telford therefore insisted on really well-made roads. First the ground had to be levelled and drained. Then a solid pavement of large stones was laid, and on top of them a layer of broken stones about the size of walnuts. Finally, to finish off, a layer of gravel up to a foot thick, so that the road should not be too hard on the feet of the Highlanders' cattle. Great care was put into drainage, for Telford was well aware of the effect of Highland rain on ill-drained roads. Great attention, too, was paid to bridges. Eleven large bridges and hundreds of small ones linked the eight hundred and seventy-five miles of road the commissioners supervised. Perhaps the finest were the iron bridges at Craigellachie and Bonar Bridge, both of which withstood batterings from logs brought down by floods when masonry bridges were swept away. By 1823 the commission had spent £267 000 of public money, as against £233 000 put up by the landowners. The result was a network of good roads, many of which were maintained by making them into turnpikes. If good communications could have saved Highland society, Telford would have provided its salvation. Unfortunately the ills lay much deeper.

Ports, docks and lighthouses

Improvements in communications were not confined to the land. Steps were also taken to improve facilities for sea-going ships calling at Scottish ports or sailing in Scottish waters. Many harbours were totally rebuilt, often at great expense, which was partly met by grants from the commissioners for forfeited estates. Once again Telford's name keeps cropping up. It was he who designed Peterhead harbour at a cost of £20 000 and spent £70 000 at Dundee between 1814 and 1825. Here his work included a floating dock and a graving dock. Between 1810 and 1814 he also completed work begun by Smeaton at Aberdeen. Other ports in the North-East, like Banff, Fraserburgh and Cullen, also benefited from his designs, but he had no hand in the rebuilding of Leith docks, which occupied the first thirty years of the nineteenth century and cost over £500 000. The work included five docks, warehouses, a drawbridge, and extensive piers and breakwaters. Thus Edinburgh had caught up on Glasgow, whose citizens

Bell Rock lighthouse. The lamp-room at the top of the tower contained twenty-four oil lamps. The flashing mechanism was controlled by clockwork.

had been investing enormous sums of money in deepening the Clyde so that ocean-going vessels could get right up to Glasgow instead of having to discharge their cargo at Port Glasgow. Smeaton, Golborne, Watt, Rennie and Telford were all consulted at one time or another between 1755 and 1807, and by dredging and building jetties the depth of water at Glasgow at high water was increased from eighteen inches in 1755 to fifteen feet in 1830. Glasgow was now a port in her own right.

Meanwhile the waters round Scotland had been made much safer by the provision of lighthouses. In 1786 there was only one Scottish lighthouse and this was on the Isle of May at the mouth of the Forth. This light had been set up in 1635 and consisted of a coal fire in a brazier on top of a stone stand. It employed three men and burned four hundred tons of coal a year. It was financed from dues paid by shipping. There were many other dangerous places needing lights, and by the end of the eighteenth century the number of ships using Scottish waters made it urgently necessary to do something. Accordingly in 1786 parliament passed an act setting up the commissioners of northern lighthouses. Their first task was to provide lighthouses at Kinnairds Head, North Ronaldsay, Eilean Glas. and the Mull of Kintyre, all of which were completed by 1789. By 1833 they had built sixteen more whose positions are shown on the map on page 65. Many were difficult to construct, but none more so than the light designed by Robert Stevenson to stand on the Bell Rock, twelve miles off the coast of Angus. The rock only shows above the water at low tide, and the task of building the tower to contain the light took from 1807 to 1811. It is a hundred and fifteen feet high and forty-two feet in diameter at the base. It weighs 2076 tons and cost about £61 000. It is the oldest rock lighthouse still working in Great Britain—a splendid tribute to its designers and builders.

Shipping and trade

The commissioners' lights guided a steadily increasing volume of shipping, for Scotland's overseas trade was growing. Up to 1776 it was based on the tobacco trade. This had begun soon after the Union, with Glasgow merchants chartering English ships to bring the leaf from the American plantations to Glasgow. Trading posts were set up and the Scottish agents worked hard to establish a good business relationship with the colonists. They succeeded, and the trade grew from 4 000 000 pounds in 1725 to 46 000 000 pounds in 1771. Most of this was re-exported to England and the continent, but the Glasgow merchants made substantial profits and the town prospered. Furthermore, goods were needed to exchange for the tobacco, and it was this need which encouraged the growth of the iron, linen and paper industries in Scotland. Then in 1776 came a great set-back with the outbreak of the War of American Independence. In 1777 the tobacco trade had dwindled to a quarter of a million pounds. Fortunately the Glasgow merchants had the capital to ride the storm and try to capture new markets with different cargoes. For a time West Indian sugar helped to keep the ships employed, but in the end it was cotton which made up the bulk of Glasgow's trade. In 1775 only 137 000 pounds of cotton had been imported. By 1812 this figure had risen to 11 000 000 pounds, and the finished cloth was being exported in Scottish ships to many parts of the continent. It was not only Glasgow which handled this commerce. Dundee and Aberdeen also had a thriving trade with the plantations.

No doubt this trade would have grown even more quickly had it not been for the dislocation caused by the Revolutionary and Napoleonic wars. Even so the expansion was sufficient to demand not only better harbours and lights but also bigger ships. Up to 1776 the biggest ship built at Greenock was one of seventy-seven tons. By 1820 ocean-going sailing ships weighing between six hundred and eight hundred tons were being built, while steam ships were being developed for the coastal trade. The first of these,

Scottish trade figures, 1760–1820

	Imports	Exports
1760	£ 850 753	£1 086 205
1770	1 213 360	1 727 918
1780	902 724	1 002 039
1790	1 688 148	1 235 405
1800	2 212 791	2 345 302
1810	3 687 133	4 741 239
1820	3 275 461	5 894 778

The paddle steamer 'Comet' like all early steam ships had sails to help economise on fuel.

the 'Comet', was built in 1812 at Port Glasgow by John Wood and Son, and carried on a successful trade until it was wrecked in 1820. By 1823 ninety-five steam boats had been built in the Clyde and Forth yards and they were now trading as far away as Ireland. This was about the limit of their range, for their engines were so inefficient that on longer journeys all their cargo space would be taken up carrying fuel. It was only after 1830 that engines were improved to make longer voyages possible.

Summing up

By 1830, then, Scotland's communications had been revolutionised to cope with the developing society. Canals and roads speeded the goods to the new harbours and lighthouses guided larger and safer ships around the coast. All this helped to make the country more prosperous. It also ended the isolation in which many Scots had lived. Journeys which had been great adventures were now commonplace. Ideas and fashions spread more quickly than before. Travel was still expensive, and the poor only benefited at second hand, but the prosperous Scot in 1830 had coach, canal

and boat services at his disposal which would have been un-
dreamed of in 1760.

What of the men who had made this possible? Landowners and
industrialists had provided much of the money. Much, too, had
come from public funds. Some of the labour came from the Highlands. Some must have come from the growing population of the
Lowland countryside. They are nameless. Not so the engineers
who provided the designs. There were not many of them. Henry
Bell designed the 'Comet'. Robert Stevenson was the first of a
family of lighthouse designers. John Rennie had a hand in canal
and harbour design. John Smeaton designed bridges and harbours
and surveyed canals. James Watt, the pioneer of steam power,
also did valuable surveying work. But above them all towered the
man whom Robert Southey christened the 'Colossus of Roads',
Thomas Telford. When it came to civil engineering his word was
law. He supervised works all over the British Isles and in Sweden,
a task which involved incessant travel to inaccessible places, only
to be confronted with problems so intricate that no one else had
been able to solve them. It was enormously demanding. Yet his
friend Southey, the poet, envied him:

'Telford's is a happy life,' he wrote, 'everywhere making roads,
building bridges, forming canals and creating harbours—works
of sure, solid, permanent utility; everywhere employing a great
number of persons, selecting the most meritorious, and putting
them forward in the world, in his own way.'

Documents

1

George Robinson writes in 1829 in *Rural Recollections* about the roads
of Scotland as he remembers them:

Nothing can be in greater contrast than these with the highways of
modern times. Thus, in some places where there was space for taking
room, it was not spared. There may be seen four, or five, or more
tracks, all collateral to each other, as each in its turn had been
abandoned, and another chosen, and all at last equally impassable.
In wet weather they became more *lairs*, sloughs, in which the carts or

carriages had to slumper through in a half-swimming state; whilst in time of drought it was a continued jolting out of one hole into another. But as there was generally room enough and to spare, in urgent cases the travellers took a new path, insomuch that, impracticable as it may seem, they contrived to get through in one way or other. In cases where the track was confined within walls or hedges on each side, which though rather a rare circumstance, did now and then occur, as there was here no room to flinch, travellers were sadly beset, and had float through or jolt through with all the patience they could muster. In short, travelling in those times, was a laborious task, exceedingly harassing and extremely slow.

a How were goods usually carried on such roads?

b Why did it become urgently necessary to improve roads in the late eighteenth century?

c How were large-scale improvements financed and organised?

2

James Maxwell writes in 1788 in praise of the Forth–Clyde Canal:

Lo, here's two vessels built with good design,
Large and substantial, fitted out right fine
To carry passengers on this canal,
Or any other goods when haste may call:
One to go east, another to go west,
Which way soever suits the purpose best.
Here passengers with cheerfulness may go
On board hereof, above deck or below.
A pleasant passage they may here enjoy,
Divest of danger, void of all annoy;
For here a cabin in each end is found,
That doth with all conveniences abound;
One in the head, for ladies nine or ten,
Another in the stern, for gentlemen,
With fires and tables, seats to sit at ease,
That may regale themselves with what they please.

a What advantages had canals over roads for passenger traffic, particularly in the early days?

b What disadvantages were there?

c What kind of goods was the canal built to carry?

3

Sir Walter Scott wrote in 1814 after visiting the Caledonian Canal:

> Had the canal been of more moderate depth, and the burdens imposed
> upon passing vessels less expensive, there can be no doubt that the
> coasters, sloops and barks would have carried on a great trade by
> means of it. But the expense and plague of locks etc. may prevent
> these humble vessels from taking this abridged voyage, while ships
> above 20 or 30 tons will hesitate to engage themselves in the intri-
> cacies of a long lake-navigation, exposed without room for manœuvr-
> ing to all the sudden squalls of the mountainous country.

a Why did Sir Walter doubt the success of the Caledonian Canal?

b What other factors helped to cut down traffic on the canal?

4

This is an extract from Robert Southey's *Journal of a Tour in Scotland
in 1819*:

> Aberdeen. Saturday, August 28 . . . The quay is very fine, and Telford
> has carried out the pier nine hundred feet beyond the point where
> Smeaton's work terminated. This great work, which cost 100,000 L.,
> protects the entrance from the whole force of the North Sea . . . A
> ship was entering under full sail—*The Prince of Waterloo*—she had
> been to America, had discharged her cargo at London, and we now
> saw her reach her own port in safety—a joyous and delightful sight.
> The Whalers are come in, and there is a strong odour of whale oil,
> which would rejoice the heart of a Greenlander . . . The harbour dues
> of this year will exceed 8000 L. . . . Coal and lime are brought to this
> country from Sunderland, and the lime is carried many miles inland
> for dressing the land.

a Why was it necessary to improve harbours like Aberdeen?

b What commodities were traded in and out of Aberdeen?

c By what means would the lime be transported inland?

d How was the money for improving harbours raised?

5 The Highlands

The Highlands of Scotland are a broken and mountainous area lying mostly down the western side of the country. It is a difficult area to live in. There are some pockets of rich soil, but for the most part the land is steep and barren. Though palm trees will grow in sheltered spots on the coast, only the hardiest plants will survive on the mountain tops a few miles inland. Communication from one valley to another is always difficult and in winter conditions often virtually impossible. Today, except in the tourist season, the Highlands are very sparsely populated. Yet in the eighteenth century about a quarter of Scotland's population lived in this inhospitable

Inveraray Castle, home of the dukes of Argyll. It was designed before 1750 but was not completed until 1770.

The home of one of the Duke of Argyll's tenants on Islay. Like Inveraray Castle, this dates from about 1760.

region. Their traditions and way of life were quite different from those of the Lowlands.

Highland society

In the past Highland society had been organised for war. The region was inhabited by clans of fighting men who usually took the name of their chief as their own. The chief was, indeed, a figure of outstanding importance. He was the proprietor of all the clan lands. In war he led his clan into battle and in peace he administered the law on his estates, for he usually inherited the office of judge along with his lands and titles. He was also trusted as one who would protect the interests of his men whenever they were threatened. Though some of the chiefs had titles and riches their power and prestige depended not only on their wealth, but also on the number of armed followers they could lead into battle. This meant that they tended to cram as many tenants as they could onto their lands.

The administration of a chief's estate was usually in the hands of tacksmen, who were often his kinsmen. They were each granted a large area of land by the chief. In return they paid rent and had to provide a certain number of armed men when the chief required them. The tacksmen kept some of the land for themselves and rented out the rest to the clansmen, who not only paid a cash rent but also had to work the tacksmen's land and turn out to fight when called.

The clansman had somehow to wring a living from the Highland soil. He usually lived in a 'town' of about half a dozen houses surrounded by arable land laid out in run-rig. To cultivate it he used either a four-horse plough or, where the plots were small and stony, a cas chrom, which was a kind of foot plough, pushed through the soil by the man himself. Like the lowland farmer he grew either oats or barley and a little flax but Highland arable was so limited in extent and so poor in quality that it was impossible to grow enough grain to feed the population, and every year meal had to be imported from the Lowlands to make up the deficiency. Fortunately there was plenty of rough pasture and most highlanders kept a few cows along with their goats, sheep and hens. Each year a couple of the cows would be taken to some local gathering area. Then, together with others, they would be driven slowly over the long green drove roads to the great cattle trysts at Falkirk or Crieff and sold to be fattened and fed to the hungry towns of Britain. The cash from these sales paid for the meal brought in each year from the Lowlands.

This kind of farming did not provide nearly enough work to keep the Highland population busy. Some of their spare time was spent

Budget of a farm on the Barrisdale Estate

Expenditure	£	s	d
Five bolls of oats	4	0	0
Rent	5	10	0
	£9	10	0

Income	£	s	d
Five cattle sold	11	5	0

Surplus of income over expenditure   £1   15   0

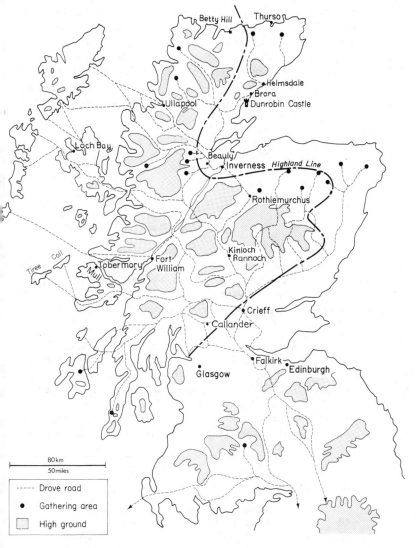

The Highland drove roads.

in processing their wool and flax into cloth, but even so they had plenty of leisure. Travellers expected them to spend at least some of this time in trying to improve the soil or bring new land into cultivation but the Highlanders knew very well that the soil was so thin and barren that such efforts would be largely wasted. They therefore preferred to spend their time in conversation and song. In the eighteenth century men were expected to be industrious, and the Highlanders were frequently criticised.

'Except as soldiers', wrote one Edinburgh gentleman, 'I question if they are fit for anything. They are the most lazy indolent miscreants I ever saw. They have no agriculture and no spur for exertion. Their great, if not their only enjoyment seems to be basking themselves in the sun during the day and singing Gaelic songs we were told over the fire in the evening. What advantage it is for a country to detain such drones as these we could not discover'.

If the Highlanders had been prosperous, outsiders would have been less upset by their apparent idleness, but they lived in miserable poverty. Their only garments were a long woollen plaid, woollen socks, brogues, and a bonnet, while according to a young Englishman their houses were

'the most miserable Hutts. They are built with Sods, the Doors are so low they are oblig'd to creep in, and windows or Holes on all sides and on the Top of the House, which serve the double purpose of letting the Light in, and the Smoke out. Near every House is a stack of Peats, a Traveller cannot distinguish the one from the other, till he comes near enough to discern the Smoke issuing from the Doors and Windows of the Dwelling-houses'.

The interiors of the houses were no better. They consisted, wrote Sarah Murray in 1799, of

'a butt, a benn and a byar; that is, a kitchen, an inner room and a place in which to put cattle. In the centre of the gavel end of the butt is heaped up dirt and stones, in which is fixed small iron bars; leaving a hollow by way of grate, with a hob

The cramped interior of a humble Highland home as seen by Thomas Pennant. Note the large family, the crude furniture and the loom. The hens seem to live in the rafters.

on each side: there is also a crank that moves any way, to which is hooked the meikle pot. There is no resemblance of a chimney, but the hole at the top; so that the whole side of the gavel is covered with soot from the side to the vent. The dirt floor is full of holes, retaining whatever wet or dirt may be thrown upon it; consequently it is always a mire. In one corner is a box nailed to the partition, between the butt and the benn. This box opens with a door in front, in which is a heath or other bed, with a great number of blankets. Into this box creep as many as it can hold; and thus they sleep, boxed in on every side, except the small door at the front.'

The only artificial light in such a house came from pieces of bog fir thrown on to the peat fire to make a blaze.

Other travellers confirmed this description. Dorothy Wordsworth wrote of the beams in Highland houses being 'crusted over and varnished' by the smoke till 'they were as glossy as black rocks on a sunny day cased in ice', while Edward Burt noted that the Highlanders themselves had sore eyes and were 'almost as black as chimney sweeps.' But his chief concern was that in dry weather the worms in the turf roof might drop down into some dish he was eating.

The Highland problem

By the eighteenth century Highland society and its values were clearly out of date. The clan chiefs, aware of the increasing prosperity of Lowland landowners, were anxious to increase the income from their estates and gradually tacksmen were replaced by professional agents, new crops were introduced and rents were raised. Until the middle of the century progress was slow and the 1745 rebellion, which brought a Highland army to within a hundred and fifty miles of London, showed clearly enough how the Highlands could still pose a threat to law and order. It is no wonder, therefore, that once the rebellion was crushed the authorities decided that this barbaric area must be brought into line with the rest of the country. The Highlands were to be made peaceful, loyal, prosperous and industrious. It was recognised that this would be a long and difficult process, but the government proved to be prepared to play its part both by direct action and by encouraging private effort.

Official policy

The government's first actions were designed to destroy the clans as fighting units. It was made illegal to demand military service in return for land and the clansmen were stripped of their arms. In addition, the power of the chiefs was reduced by abolishing the system of inheriting judicial offices, while in an attempt to break clan spirit even the wearing of highland dress was forbidden. Meanwhile some of the land of those chiefs who had joined in the rebellion was taken over and administered by commissioners appointed by the government.

These Commissioners, who administered land in thirty parishes, set to work to try to bring their estates up to date. They believed that before any progress could be made the Highlanders needed good examples to follow. Accordingly they settled soldiers and sailors returning home after the Seven Years War on their estates. They granted them land, a house and some money and hoped that they would prosper and that the Highlanders would learn from them how to make a good living from the land. Unfortunately the experiment failed. Many of the men were unsuited to such pioneering work and the others were soon discouraged by the rigours of the Highland soil and climate and left. If example failed, then schooling might succeed, and the Commissioners built schools and employed teachers. Most of them concentrated on teaching children to speak and write English and to be loyal Protestants, but a few were set up specially to teach spinning so that the Highland children would be able to earn an honest living in the textile industry.

In order to employ such labour the Commissioners tried to expand the linen industry in the Highlands. They established new settlements at Beauly and Kinloch Rannoch and built a factory at Callander. They paid grants to those setting up in business and encouraged skilled workers to come to teach their trades. Their efforts bore some fruit, for the amount of linen manufactured in the Highlands increased three-fold between 1750 and 1780. But most of this increase was on the fringes of the Highlands, in Perthshire and round Inverness. The really remote areas which needed industry most still had little. Improved communications might have helped, and the Commissioners spent a lot of money from their estates on building bridges, ranging from a few pounds for crude timber structures on remote Highland tracks to £13 000 towards the cost of Smeaton's great Tay Bridge at Perth. They also pioneered new roads in the far west, but in spite of their efforts communications in the Highlands were still poor.

The Commissioners' main efforts, however, were concentrated on improving the practice of farming on the estates which they had to administer. They sent detailed instructions to the factors who were responsible for the day-to-day running of the estates. The tenants were to be encouraged to enclose their land, build new houses and sow new crops such as grass and clover. In addition, the Commissioners provided young trees and acorns for planting on their estates. Factors were expected to send detailed reports of progress back to the Commissioners, and some of them complained that they were too tightly controlled. Be that as it may, the Annexed Estates produced good revenues, which were largely spent on improving communications. But from 1784 onwards they were one by one handed back to the families of their original owners.

Other official bodies concerned with the Highlands tended to follow broadly the same policies as the Commissioners. It was generally agreed that the Highlands could be made prosperous and civilised only if communications and agriculture were improved, villages and schools founded and industry encouraged. Chapter Four shows how the government made a determined effort to open up the Highlands by means of roads and canals, while the work of the SSPCK in founding schools in the region is discussed in Chapter Seven. Attempts were also made to encourage the herring industry.

This was done in two ways. In the first place the government organised a system of paying bounties to boats engaged in herring fishing. This did not really help the Highlanders much, however, as only large decked boats qualified for payment, and most Highlanders could only afford small open boats. The British Fisheries Society, a body composed of nobility and gentry, tackled the problem from a different angle. Founded in 1786, they tried to set up new settlements where the inhabitants would be expected to get most of their living from fishing. Villages were accordingly established at Ullapool, Tobermory and Loch Bay. The experiment failed, for the inhabitants at Ullapool and Loch Bay preferred farming to fishing, while Tobermory prospered as a trading port rather than as a fishing centre. The only place where the Society enjoyed any real success was at Wick, where they built a new harbour and a bridge across the river. Once again attempts to establish industry in remote areas in the west had failed, while money invested in an existing centre paid good dividends.

Private enterprise

Side by side with the official bodies, many Highland landowners had also been working hard, though with little capital, to make their estates more up-to-date and profitable. Many of them introduced the potato as a crop, for it yielded a good return even on poorish soil and required little skill to cultivate it. Whenever it was grown, the supply of food increased. This did little good, however. The population was increasing and as it was now possible to get a living from a smaller piece of land, the Highlanders simply reduced the size of their holdings and squeezed more people onto the land. Thus all were as poor as before, and still could not afford to pay the landowner an economic rent.

Towards the end of the century, however, the outlook for some Highland landowners improved. Cattle prices were high, rising from about thirty shillings in 1760 to £5 or £6 in 1800. In addition money could be made in the West by gathering and burning kelp, a kind of seaweed. The ash which resulted was a rich source of alkali used in the manufacture of soap and glass. The wars at the end of the eighteenth and beginning of the nineteenth century made it difficult to import alkali, and the kelp industry flourished. Usually the weed was cut with a sickle and hook. Ponies then dragged it to a beach to be dried and burnt in a primitive kiln fired by peat. The actual firing was a process requiring skill and experience. The blazing weed was stirred with long iron tools called 'clatts', and when it fused into a kind of paste it was cooled and ready to market. The marketing was done by the landowner, who arranged for an agent to transport his kelp to a convenient industrial centre for sale. Output soared and so did the price. By 1810 good quality kelp was fetching as much as £20 per ton. Of this the man who gathered and burned it could expect between £2 and £3. If he was lucky he might make four tons in a season. Thus he gained between £8 and £12 a year. Kelp burning needed a lot of labour, and so in those areas where a lot of kelp was burned landowners tended to encourage their tenants to stay, and even tried to increase

Kelp production	
1750	None
1770	2000 tons
1790	5000 tons
1810	7000 tons

their numbers. So far as they were concerned their problems seemed at an end.

Most of the landowners who made money out of kelp used it to pay off old debts or simply spent it as it came in. It was uncommon for much money to be ploughed back into the estate. Only the very rich could afford to try to develop a Highland estate along modern lines. One such was the Countess of Sutherland, who owned a vast estate in the far north. She married the Marquis of Stafford, one of the richest men in Britain, and they decided to improve their Highland estate. They sought the best advice, and were told that the soil and climate of the Highland interior was unsuitable for arable farming and for cattle rearing. To make the best use of the land the interior ought to be given over to sheep rearing under the control of a few professional shepherds, while the Highland peasants should be moved to villages on the coast where fishing and other industries could be developed.

Such ideas were not new. As early as 1791 Sir John Sinclair had argued that if the Cheviot sheep replaced cattle all over the Highlands, the area could produce wool worth £900 000 as against cattle worth £300 000. What was new was the possibility of testing out these ideas on a large scale. The Sutherlands set to work with a will. Roads were made and fishing communities like Helmsdale and Bettyhill were set up. Industrial sites were planned, based partly on the coal mine at Brora and partly on an expected expansion in the wool and linen trades. Meanwhile the peasants were cleared from their glens, and the sheep moved in to take their place. These clearances and others like them were to become notorious.

Legally there was no difficulty. A peasant's expired lease was not renewed and he was given notice to quit. To ensure that the peasants left, houses were pulled down or burned. The householder had the right to take away the roof timbers or, if they were burned, was entitled to cash compensation. Otherwise he simply gathered his few possessions and, together with his family, drove his beasts to his new home. At best the peasants were bewildered and resentful. They had been brought up to expect their clan chief to be their protector, and now it was he who was evicting them. 'I have paid sixty-six rents to the MacDonalds,' said one old man on Skye, 'and I am not one farthing in arrears. To be cast out of my house and my home to make room for his sheep is what I never expected. It is breaking my heart'. Those who carried out the evictions often had little or no sympathy with the peasants. Patrick Sellar, one of the Countess of Sutherland's agents, described the Highlanders as 'barbarous hordes' while their way of life struck him as 'sneaking indolence'. His conduct at evictions was said to have been unnecessarily brutal, and in 1816 he was tried for culpable homicide after two old people had died following an eviction in Strathnaver. He was found not guilty but the case received much publicity and there was a good deal of sympathy for the tenants who were, it seemed, being robbed of their homes and livelihoods simply to enable their landlords to become richer.

Most landowners tried to provide alternative accommodation for their tenants usually, as in Sutherland, on the coast where farming, fishing and kelp were expected to provide a livelihood. But they did not prosper. Men used to life in the glens did not adapt easily to fishing and had no great skill in arable farming. With the end of the war in 1815, moreover, prices fell. Cattle dropped from £6 to £3 10s. each and kelp from £20 to £3 a ton. Then the coastal fishing industry collapsed when the herring suddenly deserted their usual haunts. Finally the yield of potatoes began to fall as disease spread among the over-cropped potato patches. Life was still mere subsistence. But it was not only those who had been cleared who suffered. Those who remained in the glens trying to carry on with their traditional life were just as badly off, if not worse. Even the landowners found themselves no better

Highland rents

	1760	1780	1790	1810
Breadalbane (Perthshire)		£3500		£ 7700
Dunvegan		1000	£2000	7000
Reay	£500		1000	10 000

This table shows the dramatic rise in rents on three Highland estates between 1760 and 1810.

off. Rents from the Sutherland estates increased from £5 000 in 1803 to £20 000 in 1816, but even so in this period the family spent £130 000 more on the estates than they received and in succeeding years income fell short of expenditure by about £3 000 a year.

Emigration

Clearly, the highland problem had not been solved. Many landowners sold their estates to avoid bankruptcy, and many tenants decided to emigrate to Canada or America. Such a voyage proved dangerous, and those who undertook it were often ill-prepared. This was partly because dishonest shipowners competed to cash in on the situation. Advertisements like that below appeared in Scottish newspapers, and intending passengers were sometimes told that the voyage would take only eight or nine weeks, and were encouraged to take just enough food for that length of time. In fact it was often twelve or thirteen weeks before the vessel reached its destination, so that for four weeks the emigrants either starved

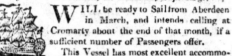

FOR PICTOU DIRECT,

THE FINE BRIGANTINE

GOOD INTENT,

Of 220 Tons burden, E. HIBBARD, *Supercargo,*

WILL be ready to Sail from Aberdeen in March, and intends calling at Cromarty about the end of that month, if a sufficient number of Passengers offer.

This Vessel has most excellent accommodation for Passengers, and Mr. Hibbard, the Supercargo, will pay them every attention.

The Fares are as follow, and payable at going on board :—

Cabin passengers .... 10 Guineas each
Steerage ditto .... 7 Guineas each
Ditto from 7 to 14 years old... 5 Guineas each
Ditto from 2 to 7 years old..... 3 Guineas each
Infants go free.

For further particulars, apply to *Alex.* and *James Gibbon, Aberdeen,* or *Charles Jameson and Sons, Inverness.*

An early application from those who intend going by the GOOD INTENT is requested, that the Owners may determine whether the Vessel shall call at Cromarty.

The interior of an emigrant ship. Many were much more cramped than this.

or bought provisions from the captain at an inflated price. The ships were often overcrowded, which led to discomfort, disease and even death. In some cases emigrants had less room than did slaves. This was because slave ships were controlled by law while emigrant ships were not. Thus the 'Sarah' and the 'Dove' sailed from Fort William in 1801 carrying seven hundred passengers. Had they been slaves the total permissible number would have been fewer than five hundred. The sufferings of those on board were dreadful. Finally the government was alerted and passed acts, the first in 1803, limiting the number of passengers and laying down a minimum quantity of provisions per head. At first the acts were difficult to enforce, for many of the boats left from remote parts where there were no officers to inspect them. Thus the sufferings continued. Nor did they end when the emigrants reached North America, for life was often very hard for the pioneers. Yet for all their difficulties they were destined to build a more prosperous society than that which they left behind.

Documents

1 *The Tiree Estate*

Tiree was owned by the Duke of Argyll. The fifth duke, who succeeded
to the title in 1770, controlled Tiree through his Chamberlain to whom
he sent detailed instructions. In 1794 he wrote complainingly:

> Tiry is a fertile island which at all times yielded a considerable rent
> for its crops and cattle before such a thing as kelp was known or
> heard of in that quarter.
>
> The present rent of Tiry is about £1000, and there was this year
> sold from it 159 tons of kelp, at four guineas the ton amounting to
> £677, and allowing half of this sum to go to the tenants for their
> labour in making it, the other half being £338: 10/- seems fairly to
> belong to me, which being taken from the total rent of £1000 leaves
> about £640 to be paid out of the Island consisting of 13 000 acres of
> fertile land.
>
> I cannot think that this return, which is less than one shilling the
> acre, is what in reason and in justice I ought to expect for such land.
>
> From one end of Britain to the other farmers in general pay their
> rents either with their wheat crops where wheat is raised, or with their
> barley crops where there is no wheat. You admit that the island grows
> 1000 bolls of barley yearly, and I know every boll which the farmer
> chooses to sell yields to him at least twenty shillings, so that after
> allowing the tenants to retain one third for seed, I should get above
> £600 from this article yearly.
>
> I know a number of cattle are reared and that a considerable addi-
> tion to the rent can and ought to be made from that article.
>
> I allow all the oats, all the potatoes, all the lint, all the sheep, all the
> milk, butter, cheese, poultry, eggs, fish etc., which in other countries
> are sold for payment of the landlord's rent. I allow all these to go for
> the support of the tenants because I wish them to live happily and
> plentifully.
>
> From these observations I am satisfied that betwixt kelp, barley
> and cattle, I ought to receive from the island far beyond the present
> rent.

The Chamberlain replied thus:

> The population of Tiry is daily increasing and at present amounts
> nearly to 2500 souls, and as they have no other means of support, but
> from the produce of the land, they must of course consume a great
> part of it within themselves, besides what must be laid out in paying
> servants' wages, and procuring the other necessaries they stand in

need of. The island produces scarce any wool, and that article alone will require a considerable sum of money. The tenants are in general much crowded, and few of them in circumstances to occupy much land.

The price of both cows and stotts is from one third to one fourth below what such cattle bred in Mull or Coll usually sell for, which together with the difficulty in disposing of them discourages the tenants from paying much attention to the rearing of cattle. Barley is generally sold from 16/- to 18/- p. boll, and only in cases of extreme scarcity exceeds the latter price, so that the factor thinks 17/- a fair average for it. There are scarce any horses sold out of the island, and tho' some farms sell a few, it does not add to the general produce, and a considerable number are yearly imported from Mull and Coll. The island is not found to answer for sheep, and very few are reared there.

The Tiry kelp generally sells from 5/- to 10/- p. ton below the Mull prices and the expence of manufacturing it is not less than £2 p. ton.

a Does anything in his complaints suggest that the Duke was not familiar with Highland farming conditions? If so, what?

b Which do you find more convincing: the Duke's complaints or the Chamberlain's reply? Give reasons for your decision.

c Was the division of the proceeds from kelp typical?

d Which problems on Tiree, as outlined in the Chamberlain's report, were typical of the Highlands as a whole, and which peculiar to the island and others like it?

N.B. By 1831 the population of Tiree had risen to 4453. It is now less than 1000.

2 The clearances

In 1820 Mr. James Loch, general agent of the Sutherland Estates, published a pamphlet explaining why the clearances were in the best interests of the country. This is an extract from it:

It had long been known, that the coast of Sutherland abounded with many different kinds of fish, not only sufficient for the consumption of the country, but affording also a supply *to any extent* for more distant markets or for exportation, when cured and salted. Besides the regular and continual supply of white fish, with which the shores thus abound, the coast of Sutherland is annually visited by one of those vast shoals of herrings, which frequent the coast of Scotland. It seemed as it if had been pointed out by Nature, that the system for this remote district, in order that it might bear its suitable importance in contributing its share to the general stock of the country, was, to convert the mountainous districts into sheep walks, and to remove the inhabitants to the coast, or to the valleys near the sea.

It will be seen that the object to be obtained by this arrangement was two-fold: it was, in the first place, to render this mountainous district contributory, as far as it was possible, to the general wealth and industry of the country, and in the manner most suitable to its situation and peculiar circumstances. This was to be effected by making it produce a large supply of wool, for the staple manufactury of England. While at the same time, it should support as numerous, and a far more laborious and useful population, than it hitherto had done at home: and in the second place, to convert the inhabitants of those districts to the habits of regular and continued industry, and to enable them to bring to market a very considerable surplus quantity of provisions, for the supply of the large towns in the southern parts of the island, or for the purpose of exportation.

A Sutherland clergyman gave a different point of view:

Ancient respectable tenants, who passed the greater part of life in the enjoyment of abundance, and in the exercise of hospitality and charity, possessing stocks of ten, twenty and thirty breeding cows, with the usual proportion of other stock, are now pining on one or two acres of bad land, with one or two starved cows, and, for this accommodation a calculation is made, that they must support their families and pay the rent of their lots, which the land cannot afford. When the herring fishery (the only fishery prosecuted on this coast) succeeds, they generally satisfy the landlords, whatever privations they may suffer, but when the fishing fails, they fall in arrears, and are sequestrated, and their stock sold to pay the rents, their lots given to others, and they and their families turned adrift on the world.

a What other reasons, not mentioned by Mr. Loch, were there for bringing in sheep?
b In what ways is the picture painted by the clergyman of life before the clearances not typical?
c What went wrong with the scheme for fishing outlined by Mr. Loch?
d What evidence is there that both writers are trying to 'make a case' rather than give an unbiased account?

6 Politics

The electoral system

After 1707 Scotland was no longer a political unit. It was now 'North Britain'—the mere 'knuckle-end of England'. True, it kept its own law, its own church and, for a year, its own Privy Council. But its parliament was gone. Instead it was represented by sixteen Scottish peers in the House of Lords and by forty-five members in the House of Commons. The sixteen peers were elected by the whole of the Scottish nobility at Holyrood House every time there was a general election. Those who chose not to attend could appoint proxies to vote in their places. This sounds fair and democratic, but in fact the government in London sent down a list of those it wished to be chosen and could always rely on getting its way. This was because most of the nobility either received or hoped to receive a government post or pension, and therefore hastened to vote for those whom the government approved. The lucky sixteen then set out for London where, by supporting the government, they hoped for more important posts and increased influence. They were rarely disappointed.

So much for the Lords. The situation of those in the Commons was more complicated in that forty-five members had to be shared among thirty-three counties and sixty-six royal burghs, which had all returned members to the Scottish parliament. It was decided that the twenty-seven largest counties should be given one member each, while the other six would be represented in every alternate parliament. Among the burghs Edinburgh alone had a member of its own. All the others were grouped into fourteen districts, each containing either four or five burghs. Each district returned one member (see map on next two pages).

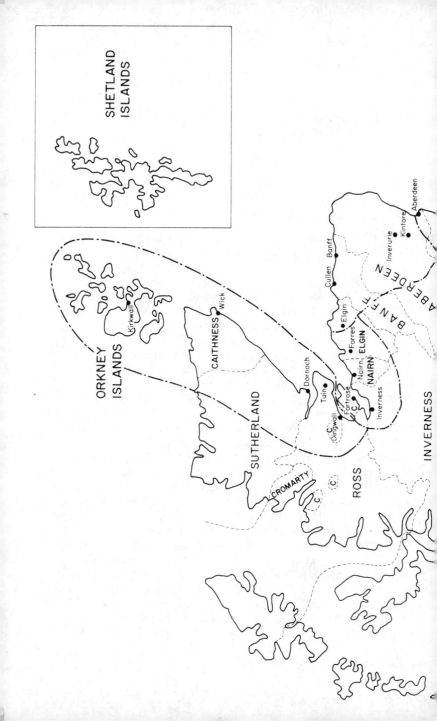

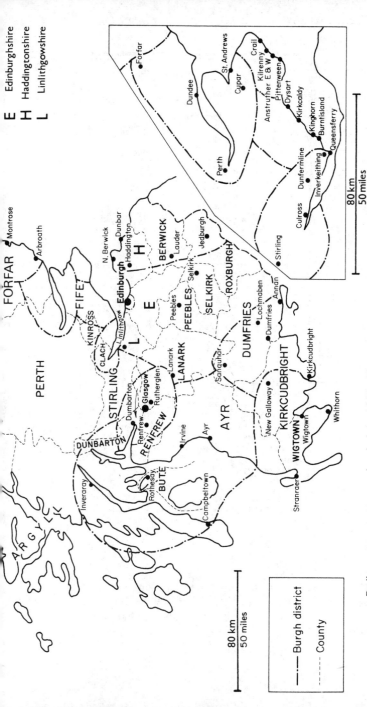

E Edinburghshire
H Haddingtonshire
L Linlithgowshire

Parliamentary representation before 1832. The paired counties (see page 99) were Nairn and Cromarty, Clackmannan and Kinross, and Bute and Caithness. Orkney and Shetland made up one county, but Shetland never had anyone qualified to vote.

Burgh district
County

Aberdeen.
July 28.

The election of a Member of Parliament for this county took place here on the 23d curt. The candidates were JAMES FERGUSON, Esq. of *Pitfour*, our late representative, and MAJOR GENERAL HAY of *Rannes*, when Mr Ferguson was re-elected by a majority of votes.——The numbers were, 61 to 41.

MR FERGUSON begs leave to offer his most grateful acknowledgements to his Friends who did him the honour of such respectable support at the late Election for this County.

He trusts they will believe, that he never can forget the very great obligation they have conferred on him; and that a steady attention to the best interests of the Country, and in particular to those of the County of Aberdeen, will ever actuate his conduct in Parliament.

TO THE
FREEHOLDERS *of the County of* ABERDEEN.

MAJOR GENERAL HAY begs leave to return his sincere thanks to those Gentlemen of the County of Aberdeen, who did him the honour to support him on Friday last. He will ever retain the most grateful recollection of their friendship.

Major General Hay takes the liberty to add, that as he brought forward his pretensions at the desire of a number of respectable friends, so he is resolved, in his future conduct, to be guided entirely by their opinion. Meanwhile, he entreats that his friends in general will enter into no engagement.

ABERDEEN, *July 26th,* 1802.

A newspaper report of the Aberdeenshire election of 1802 with statements by the two candidates. The number of votes was about average for the county.

County elections

There were, in fact, few contested elections. In the counties only landowners could vote. In 1823 it was reckoned that the total county electorate for Scotland was about 3000. There were fewer than twenty-five electors in Caithness, about a hundred in Mid-lothian and about double that number in Ayrshire. Under these circumstances the electors could easily meet informally long before the election and decide who was to be their member. As a rule the choice was in any case automatic, for most areas had their dominant families who owned so much land and had so much power that they all but nominated the member. Such were the Gordons in Aberdeenshire and the Hamiltons in Lanarkshire. Dif-ficulties arose only where two such families were competing for the same county. Thus between 1790 and 1810 the Earl of Fife, who controlled Banffshire, tried to take over Aberdeenshire as well. The result was a series of contested elections in which the Duke of Gordon succeeded in holding off the Earl's challenge. In 1806 it was a close thing, for General Hay, the Fife candidate, actually controlled more votes than Ferguson of Pitfour who represented the Gordon interest. The day was saved by the chairman of the meeting who refused to poll six of Hay's supporters on the grounds that they were not properly qualified.

It was, indeed, likely enough that some of the voters had no qualifications. Scottish land law was very complicated and it was common practice for local magnates to 'create' freeholds. That is to say they would give some of their reliable tenants a 'wadsett', or mortgage, which made them, in law, the owners of their lands, thereby entitling them to vote. Thus the Duke of Gordon wrote to his factor, William Tod, in 1773:

Sir,

I shall consider it as a particular favour if you will be so oblidging as to accept of a Qualification in Inverness-shire upon the terms of a wadsett for life of the superiorities and Feu duties of lands in the County, having the highest confidence in your friendship and regard for me and my family, I am, with regard, Sir,

Your most obedient humble servant,
Gordon.

Such a qualification was no doubt legal and, when he had held it for a year, entitled William Tod to vote in Inverness county elections as a free and independent landowner. But sometimes there was a more urgent need of voters, as in 1806, when William Tod wrote to Charles Gordon:

> his grace wishes you to think immediately of getting qualifications provided for Lord Alexander Gordon and Colonel George Gordon in Aberdeenshire . . . It is understood they are to be good sound constitutional qualifications, and in perpetuity.

It was often difficult to get such qualifications quickly, and when they were obtained, they were carefully examined by the other side in case there was anything wrong with them. It is no wonder that most of the time at county elections was spent in arguing about whether those present were really entitled to vote and very little in considering the merits of the candidates.

Burgh elections

In burgh elections the situation was, if anything, worse, with bribery rampant. Normally the council for each burgh in a group appointed a delegate. The delegates then met and elected the member for the district. A Scots lawyer, Henry Cockburn, wrote of the results of this district system:

> Instead of bribing the town-councils, the established practice was to bribe only the delegates, or indeed only one of them, if this could secure the majority. Not that the councils were left unrefreshed, but that the hooks with the best bait were set for the most effective fish.

If an election was contested, then the burgh councils could expect a rich harvest of bribes. In an election for the northern group of burghs Mr. Craigie's agent was advised to tell his candidate

> that he must give three, or four Hundred Pound to the Town of Dingwall to make his election quite sure considering Sir Robert [the other candidate] is content to give Two Thousand.[1] Insist hard with Craigie, what is it to one who gets 1500 a year?

Apparently Mr. Craigie paid up, for he was duly elected.

[1] This sum was probably mentioned to frighten Mr. Craigie. If Sir Robert had really offered £2000, he would most likely have won the election.

Results of the system

Two points need to be made about this system. The first is that the members elected under it did not really represent their country at all. The only voters were a few corrupt town councillors and a couple of thousand country gentry. The vast mass of the people were not involved. Politics were not their concern and, indeed, they paid little attention to them. Only at a time of great crisis did they feel a sense of grievance at being completely ignored and try to do something about it. The second point is that with so few electors it was possible for one powerful man by hard work to dominate the whole system, to ensure that most Scottish members owed their election to his influence and would vote as he wished. Such a man, who might control as many as forty votes in the House of Commons, would be in a position to dictate terms to almost any government and might hope for one of the great offices of state. Lord Islay, afterwards Duke of Argyll, gained control of enough seats in the middle of the eighteenth century to ensure that any government which ignored him did so at their peril, but the man who succeeded in exploiting the Scottish electoral system to the full was Henry Dundas, afterwards Viscount Melville.

The Career of Dundas

Dundas was an intelligent, hard-working, level-headed man. He was approachable and good-natured and was capable of inspiring loyalty in those about him, though he could be ruthless when occasion demanded. So far as religion was concerned he was tolerant, so long as it did not threaten to upset society or interfere with politics. He was as honest as most politicians of his day, and much more efficient than many. His real driving force was a love of power, a determination to get and keep a position of real influence and authority. He had no schemes to use such a position to introduce sweeping reforms for the benefit of his fellow-men. He sought power because he enjoyed it.

He did not come from one of the great landed families of Scotland. The Dundases were Midlothian gentry who tended to become lawyers. Henry, born in 1742, duly became an advocate, but at the age of twenty-four was made Solicitor-General for Scotland, probably through the influence of his half-brother who was Lord President of the Court of Session. In 1774 he was elected MP for Midlothian and in 1775 was made Lord Advocate. He was efficient and loyal but came to the conclusion that the Prime Minister, Lord North, did not place a high enough value on his services. What was more, it became clear that North's ministry was being undermined by the success of the American colonists in their revolt against British rule. Slowly Dundas loosened the ties binding him to North while at the same time using his position as Lord Advocate to extend his influence over the Scottish electoral machinery. Landowners found him always ready to oblige, recommending them or their relations for pensions and posts. In return they listened to him when he suggested who should become a member of parliament, and how he should vote. By 1780 he controlled twelve seats, and by 1783 he had transferred his allegiance from Lord North to William Pitt, who became Prime Minister at twenty-four, facing a multitude of problems.

One of the greatest of these was that of India. Here Dundas was able to be a great help, for he had made a deep study of the

This is the least flattering portrait of Henry Dundas. It may well also be the best likeness.

problem himself and was largely responsible for drawing up the India Bill which Pitt put forward to settle the relationship between the East India Company and the British government. It set up a Board of Control with enormous powers and it was quite natural that Dundas should become a member of that board. This at once vastly increased his power, for he now had a huge range of posts in India to dispose of. He was flooded with applications and he tended to appoint those who, as well as doing an efficient job, could help him extend his control over Scotland's MPs. By the end of 1784 he controlled twenty-two seats. His power was now secure and continued to grow. He proved an efficient administrator and it was clear that the Prime Minister would usually listen to his advice on the suitability of Scotsmen for posts and pensions. There was nobody to compete with him. More and more landowners made bargains with him and by 1790 he controlled thirty-four seats. Later he was made Home Secretary and then Secretary of State for War. In 1802 he was created Viscount Melville. It was not until 1806 that he fell from power.

Few well-to-do Scotsmen resented Dundas's authority. In a way they were proud of his success and grateful that he did his best to help the careers of his fellow-countrymen. Even when he refused their requests they did not necessarily turn against him. Thus in 1788 Cosmo Gordon of Cluny wrote in a letter to a friend:

> I ask't a small pension for Mrs. Ross from Mr. Dundas, but notwithstanding his absolute power and our early intimate and uniform friendship it has not been granted; . . . tho I was disappointed it was too small a matter and too easily supplyable for me to complain of the refusal, or to lessen in my esteem the Person who governs with equal ability and Success the Nabobs of India and the Peers of the North of Scotland.

Dundas, it seemed, could do no wrong. As long as he was in control Scotland's political system worked smoothly enough, regularly delivering its consignment of members who, though occasionally liable to have a will of their own on Scottish matters, could always be relied on to support the government on everything else. They did not need to listen to the debates, but simply voted every time on the same side as the Lord Advocate who, according to

Ferguson of Pitfour, had to be a tall man. 'We Scotch members', he is said to have remarked, 'always vote with him, and we need, therefore, to be able to see him.'

The early reformers

There were, however, those who thought the system needed reform. In 1768 Lord Buchan protested that the election of the representative peers was 'a mere ministerial nomination, at once disgraceful to the community and subversive to the freedom of parliament'. Nothing was changed as a result of his protests. There was also a drive by the country gentry against the creation of freeholds solely for the purpose of making new votes in county elections. They felt angry at this practice because it lowered the status of their own genuine qualifications. The Court of Session supported them partly because of the legal difficulties created by the falsification of records which was an inevitable part of the practice. In 1782 there was a meeting attended by representatives of twenty-three counties out of a total of thirty-three. Those present embarked on a campaign to clean up county elections. But there were too few of them and they were working against the interests of the nobility. Thus, though the county electoral rolls were examined in 1790 and many unqualified voters removed from them, in the long run they had little effect.

The same was true of efforts to reform the burghs. The councils who had absolute control over town affairs were usually self-electing. That is to say that when a vacancy occurred, the councillors themselves decided who should fill it. The other inhabitants had nothing at all to do with it. Most councils were dishonest, using public funds for personal profit. Bribery and inefficiency were rampant. Many tradesmen and manufacturers were prospering at this time, and felt that they too were entitled to a say in how their town was run. In some burghs a number of them were voted on to the councils. In others the old gang rigorously excluded them and did nothing to encourage industry. At the end of 1782 an Edinburgh man, Thomas McCrugar, wrote a series of articles for the *Caledonian Mercury*. In these, called the 'Letters of Zeno', he argued that all the 'men in the middle ranks of life' ought to have some part in running their town. He won a lot of support among merchants and lawyers, and in March 1784 a convention met in Edinburgh at which thirty-three of the sixty-six royal burghs were represented. This convention proposed that all resident burgesses should have a vote in burgh elections, and should appoint auditors to see that the accounts were properly kept. They framed their proposals into a bill, but none of the Scottish members would touch it. In the end it was introduced by Richard Sheridan, although Dundas saw to it that it made no progress.

None of these reformers had wanted to make any very sweeping changes in the Scottish electoral system. Even McCrugar, whose ideas on burgh reform were far-reaching, expressly excluded working people from having the vote. Describing them as 'the dregs of the population', he thought them 'disqualified by ignorance and hebetude'.[1] But there were others with different ideas and their voices were being heard more and more in Scotland. As early as 1776 the founders of the USA proclaimed their belief that all men were entitled to 'life, liberty and the pursuit of happiness', and in the same year John Wilkes told the House of Commons that 'the meanest mechanic, the poorest peasant and day labourer' had the right to a say in how he was governed. But America was a long way away and Wilkes was a crank. Few took his suggestion seriously. It was a different matter when England's neighbour France, the most powerful monarchy in the world, was suddenly shattered by a revolution which proclaimed that all men had equal rights.

The effects of the French Revolution

Burke and Paine

To begin with most people in Britain welcomed the revolution, if only because it seemed that it must put Britain's greatest rival out of action for a while. Most, too, were genuinely pleased that a despotic monarchy had been swept away and hoped that something on British lines would replace it. Only a few were uneasy,

[1] Idleness.

and one of them, Edmund Burke, decided to publish his *Reflections on the Revolution in France*. The book appeared in 1790. In it Burke condemned the revolution root and branch. Sweeping away a system of government which had existed for centuries only to replace it by one controlled by the 'swinish multitude' would, he warned, lead to chaos, war and a military dictatorship. Those in Britain with property and power to lose lost their enthusiasm for events in France and began fearfully to look for signs of a similar outbreak in Britain. They had not long to wait, for in 1791 Tom Paine, an Englishman who had lived in America, published *The Rights of Man*—an answer to Burke.

Paine was an extremist—a republican. And he took care to make his position clear. 'The Monarchy', he said, 'is the master-fraud which shelters all others'. Again the 'constitution' which Burke so admired 'is a bad Constitution for at least ninety-nine parts of the nation out of a hundred'. As for the nobility they were parasites. 'The Aristocracy', he wrote, 'are not the farmers who work the land . . . but are the mere consumers of the rent.' The whole society needed to be swept away and replaced by one in which taxation was to be taken from the rich for the benefit of the needy. *The Rights of Man* was an alarming work and it appeared at a time when events in France were beginning to go exactly the way that Burke had foretold. Worse still it proved enormously popular. In spite of being condemned as a seditious libel in 1792 it sold above 200 000 copies by the end of the year. It sold particularly well in Scotland for it pointed out clearly the injustice of a political system which excluded the vast majority of the population from any say in the government.

Other political writings did well too. In 1782 there were only eight newspapers in Scotland. By 1790 there were twenty-seven, almost all of them putting forward a political point of view. Dissatisfaction with the system grew. In June 1792 a mob in Edinburgh burned Dundas in effigy and one of its leaders was sentenced to fourteen years' transportation.

Government repression

This ferocious sentence was part of a deliberate policy. As the revolution in France became more and more extreme, abolishing the monarchy and imprisoning the King, so the authorities in Britain were more and more determined to stifle criticism of the British constitution and prevent demonstrations of discontent. Thus in December 1792 Paine was found guilty in his absence of seditious libel. In the same month a convention of the Friends of the People in Scotland, a moderate organisation as a rule, took place in Edinburgh. It was attended by a hundred and sixty delegates and passed motions calling for parliamentary reform. It was exactly the sort of thing the government wished to discourage. They therefore arrested the most prominent member of the convention, Thomas Muir, an advocate, who had already got into the government's black books by defending one of those condemned for the riot in which Dundas's effigy had been burned. He had also been very active in demanding reform, and at the convention had read out a very extreme address from the Society of United Irishmen. He eventually came to trial in August 1793, by which time Britain and France were at war. What was more the Friends of the People had held a second, much more extreme convention in May. Clearly an example was needed.

Muir was to provide that example. He was accused of making seditious speeches, circulating *The Rights of Man,* and reading out the notorious address of the United Irishmen with obvious approval. There were several ways of countering the charge with some hope of success, for the evidence was weak. Muir, however, made the prosecution's task easy by making a political speech instead of attacking the prosecution's case. Lord Braxfield in his summing up made the most of this. He reminded the jury of the dangerous times in which they lived and spoke of the peril of giving the lower orders the idea that they had any political rights. The government 'is made up of the landed interest, which alone has a right to be represented; as for the rabble, who have nothing but personal property, what hold has the nation of them?' Muir was found guilty and sentenced to fourteen years' transportation to Botany Bay. He was, in fact, rescued from Australia by some Americans in 1796 and eventually died in France in 1799.

In spite of Muir's condemnation and the sentence of seven years' transportation passed on Thomas Palmer, a minister in Dundee, the local Societies of the Friends of the People continued to meet, and even organised a joint meeting with the London Corresponding Society to take place in Edinburgh. This meeting was really a deliberate act of defiance, organised so that the Londoners could come up and demonstrate their sympathy with their Scottish comrades and their contempt for the men who had sentenced Muir. The convention met in November 1793. Its deliberations were secret, but when it was ordered to disperse by the authorities many of the delegates carried on. This led to many arrests and to three trials. Two of the accused, Joseph Gerrald and Maurice Margarot, were from London. The third, William Skirving, was secretary of the Canongate Society of Friends of the People. All three were sentenced to fourteen years' transportation. This time the sentences worked, for the reform societies disintegrated.

The government was, however, determined to leave nothing to chance. The English Habeas Corpus Act and the Scottish Act against Wrongous Imprisonment were both suspended. This meant that suspects could now be held in prison indefinitely without trial. As if to confirm the ministers' fears a number of pikeheads were discovered in Edinburgh. These, it was claimed, were to be used in an attempt to start a revolution in Scotland. Two men, Robert Watt and David Downie, were charged with high treason. Both were condemned and Watt was hanged. The 'Pike Plot' was the work of a few desperate men but the authorities exaggerated its importance, and the discovery of such weapons terrified many respectable Scots and made them lose all sense of proportion. All those who wished to alter any detail of the existing system were looked on as dangerous revolutionaries, and were liable to lose their livelihood and, if they spoke carelessly, their liberty as well. This 'revolutionary horror' lasted nearly ten years.

The volunteers and the militia

In the meantime attempts were made to meet the threat of invasion from France and that of revolution at home by the foundation of volunteer companies. These were composed of the upper and middle classes and carefully excluded any who were suspected of revolutionary sympathies. Such companies frequently had splen-

An informal drawing of
Thomas Muir.

did uniforms and drilled and exercised with great enthusiasm. By 1796 there were many volunteer companies, but in 1797 the war was going so badly that it was felt that something more was needed. Both England and Ireland had a militia into which anybody could be called to serve. Scotland had no such organisation because the rising of 1745 had made the government feel it would be dangerous to put arms indiscriminately into the hands of Scots. But in 1797 the possibility of French invasion outweighed such fears and an act was passed setting up a Scottish militia. Those selected to serve were to be paid 1s $1\frac{1}{2}$d per day and would not be asked to go overseas. If you were selected and did not wish to serve you could hire a substitute to take your place. Selection was by ballot.

So much for the act. To put it into effect needed a good deal of work. To begin with parish registers were used as a basis for selecting names, but these were incomplete and a census had to be organised. All this in addition to appointing officers and distributing arms and supplies placed a considerable burden on the authorities, who often did not bother to explain the terms of the Militia Act properly. Rumours therefore spread rapidly. Some said that those who were enlisted would be sent overseas. Others maintained that they would not be paid. Discontent grew. Parish registers were destroyed and the census was greeted by riots. The government was alarmed. The Lord Advocate blamed the radicals for the trouble, and it is true that they were quick to point out how unfair it was that a rich man selected to serve could hire a substitute while a poor man had to obey the call. But most of the trouble was caused by misunderstandings and, once the terms of the act became known, the riots largely died down.

The colliers at Tranent provided a notable exception. Looked down on by other workers, they had a very strong sense of community. What was more the militia pay was less than half their normal earnings. Thus, when some of their number were conscripted, troops had to be called from Haddington to deal with these furious miners. They had a difficult task and lost their tempers, riding through the countryside hitting out at all they encountered. Eleven people were killed, including a boy of thirteen. None of the soldiers was ever prosecuted. In spite of rather than because of such incidents, the militia was enrolled, though even as late as 1799 there was a riot against the draft among miners at Bathgate in West Lothian.

The year 1799 also saw an act suppressing radical societies. This was needed to deal with the United Scotsmen—a genuinely revolutionary organisation based on the militant United Irishmen. There were not many of them and one of their leaders, George Mealmaker, had been transported for fourteen years on a charge of sedition in 1797. But in 1798 there was a rebellion in Ireland and once again the government took no chances. Gradually the United Scotsmen fell to pieces. Disturbances became few and insignificant. The war went on. The system of government, with all its corrupt practices, functioned as usual. The challenge to its authority had been met and broken.

The Edinburgh Review

The tide began to turn after 1802. This was partly because a peace treaty was made with the French, which helped passions to cool. But even when the war was resumed in 1803 there was a much freer atmosphere than in the 1790s. Gradually the reformers took heart encouraged by a new periodical—the *Edinburgh Review*. This first appeared in October 1802 and was the idea of the Reverend Sydney Smith who edited the first number. The *Review* was a lively, independent periodical, generally on the side of reform. Its chief contributors—Smith himself, Francis Jeffrey, Francis Horner and Henry Brougham—were all relatively young men of great ability. They could write entertainingly, clearly and with apparent authority on any subject. They obviously enjoyed writing and the *Review* sold in large numbers in England as well as Scotland. Its cheerful common sense contrasted with the picture of the reformer as a crazed ruffian in a cellar manufacturing pike-heads to puncture the gentry. Then in 1805 came a major change —the resignation of Dundas. In 1804 he had been made First Lord of the Admiralty, and a year later had allowed the treasurer of the Navy to use Navy funds for private speculation. Dundas had made nothing out of this himself and, when impeached, was acquitted. He had, however, to resign and was out of office until his death in 1811.

Dundas's fall and the death of Pitt were followed by a new government in which the Whigs at last had some say. It did not last long, and, so far as Scotland was concerned, its most important act was to put forward a plan to reform the Court of Session which had long been overwhelmed with work. The government fell before the reform could be carried through, but the court was reorganised in 1808 by a Tory administration. This helped to make justice more speedy. It was also made fairer by long-overdue reforms of the jury system in 1825, and, for the first time in Scotland, by the introduction of a jury for civil cases in 1816.

The weavers' strike

Thus from 1800 to 1810 politics seemed less violent. Some of the old bitterness crept back between 1810 and 1820. This was partly due to industrial unrest, for prices were high and wages were low. Particularly hard-hit were the hand loom weavers. As their numbers increased, so their pay dropped to the absurd level of 5s a week for skilled work. In England many turned to machine-breaking. In Glasgow they discovered a statute passed in 1661 which empowered magistrates to fix fair rates of pay. They therefore petitioned the magistrates to order the employers to pay a living wage. The magistrates did so. The employers appealed to the Court of Session, which upheld the weavers' case. The employers ignored the court order. The weavers, confident that the law was on their side, went on strike. Many of their leaders were promptly arrested and imprisoned, though the most important, Alexander Richmond, fled. To make matters worse, the government repealed the 1661 act. It was an appalling piece of cheap trickery at the expense of a body of men reduced to destitution through no fault of their own.

The State Trials, 1817

The weavers were not entirely on their own. The Whig lawyers, Francis Jeffrey and Henry Cockburn, acted on their behalf in the court cases and the government's tactics in this case probably helped to account for a growth of radical activity. In 1813 some Edinburgh workers rioted and in 1814 the middle-class reformers held a vast meeting to demand the abolition of slavery. Then in 1814, to keep the pot boiling, came the seventy-five-year-old reformer, Major John Cartwright, who ever since 1776 had been urging that all men should have the vote, that members of parliament should be paid, that all constituencies should be the same size, and that there should be a general election every year. Since 1812 he had been touring England founding Hampden Clubs 'for turning the discontents into a legal channel favourable to parliamentary reform'. His tour of Scotland in 1815 was a great success and Hampden Clubs were founded in Glasgow, Dundee and Aberdeen. In 1816, as trade slackened and unemployment increased, so the workers became more and more restive.

The authorities were well aware of all this through their system of spies. By autumn 1816 Alexander Richmond, the weavers' leader, had been persuaded by Kirkman Finlay, the Glasgow cotton magnate, to report on the activities of his fellow-workers. He brought serious news. After a meeting in Glasgow addressed by Major Cartwright a number of workers had banded themselves together and taken an oath to keep their discussion secret on pain of death. This was illegal and Finlay sent the news to the Lord Advocate, Alexander Maconochie, who gave the House of Commons the impression that Glasgow was menaced by a gang of revolutionary cut-throats. It was stirring stuff and the Commons demanded the arrest and punishment of such ruffians. Accordingly the workers' leaders were arrested and brought to trial in the spring and summer of 1817.

The result was a terrible humiliation for Maconochie and for the government. The first two accused, Alexander McLaren, a weaver, and Thomas Baird, a grocer, both came from Kilmarnock. Both were respectable men who had served in the volunteers. Both admitted attending radical meetings and were accused of sedition because they had helped in the printing and publication of pamphlets. Both men were well defended and, though they were found guilty, were sentenced to only six months in prison. Sterner sentences were to be reserved for the more dangerous revolutionaries. Eventually William Edgar was brought to trial, charged with administering an illegal oath—a capital offence. Unfortunately for the prosecution Maconochie had drawn up the indictment so badly that it was at once rejected and the trial postponed. In May 1817 Neil Douglas, a Glasgow preacher, was accused of sedition. According to the Solicitor-General he had compared George III to Nebuchadnezzar and had made many other seditious remarks in the course of a sermon. The preacher, defended by Francis Jeffrey, maintained that he had been misrepresented. He had a strong Highland accent which made him difficult to understand when excited, as he frequently was when preaching. He was found not guilty. In July Andrew McKinlay, a Glasgow weaver, was put on trial like Edgar for administering an illegal oath. This time the indictment was properly framed, but the case against McKinlay collapsed when the chief prosecution witness admitted that he had been bribed to give evidence by the advocate-depute. McKinlay was acquitted.

The Radical War, 1820

So ended the State Trials of 1817. The charges against Edgar and the other prisoners were dropped. The year 1818 was quiet but in 1819 trade languished and there was more trouble, mostly in England. Edinburgh remained in Cockburn's words 'as quiet as the grave, or even as Peebles' but in the industrial West a number of radical unions sprang up. In the winter plans were made for a rising to be co-ordinated with similar outbreaks in England but the leaders of the plot were arrested in February 1820. At the beginning of April bills appeared in Glasgow calling on the people to support a new revolutionary government and the weavers went on strike. A few from Strathaven marched to the outskirts of Glasgow but finding no support went home again. Others from Calton, marching to join up with forces which they wrongly believed were coming up from England, were dispersed by a force of cavalry. In all forty-seven prisoners were taken and tried for treason. Three—James Wilson, John Baird and Andrew Hardie—were executed.

Attempts at burgh reform

Meanwhile attempts were being made to reform the Scottish royal burghs. It had long been the practice in the case of an irregular burgh election to apply to the government for a poll warrant. If such a warrant was granted, then the council could be unseated. The burgh reform association decided to make the maximum possible use of this system, even to the extent of deliberately breaking election laws themselves so that they could be sure that a cast-iron case could be made out for the issue of a poll warrant. In this way the council of Montrose was unseated in 1817. This precedent alarmed the government, for the councils controlled between them fifteen seats in the Commons. If the reformers had their way, then all these seats would be lost to the government. The remedy was simple. No more poll warrants were granted, however good the case.

Defeated in this, the burgh reformers tried another tack. In 1819 Lord Archibald Hamilton succeeded in getting a parliamentary committee appointed to investigate the Scottish burghs. When it reported, it confirmed that Edinburgh, Aberdeen, Dundee and

Dunfermline had all been bankrupted by the corruption and inefficiency of their councils. The committee also revealed that a congenital idiot had been made town clerk of Forfar, and could not legally be deprived of his office. In Cupar seats on the council were openly bought and sold, while in the North-East Colonel Francis Grant, MP, was provost of Elgin, provost of Forres, provost of Cullen and a councillor in Nairn all at the same time, in spite of a rule in three of these burghs that officials had to be resident merchants. Thus the government was exposed as defending a dishonest system.

Yet the system still stood. It was not until the Tory party fell to pieces over Catholic emancipation that there was at least a chance of reform. Even in 1830 when the Whigs won a majority in England, Scotland still returned a majority of Tories. Though battered and discredited the machinery creaked on until dismantled by the reform act of 1832 while the burghs were reformed in 1833. For most of the rest of the nineteenth century Scotland voted Liberal. No other comment need be made on the Tory rule from 1760 to 1830 and its effect on Scottish opinion.

Documents

1

In a letter to his brother in June 1794, Francis Jeffrey describes the political situation in Scotland:

. . . There are three parties, I think, distinguishable enough. The first, which is the loudest, and I believe the most powerful, is that of the fierce aristocrats—men of war, with their swords and their rank—men of property, with their hands on their pockets, and their eyes staring wildly with alarm and detestation—men of indolence and morosity, and withal, men of place and expectation. The desperate democrats are the second order—numerous enough too, and thriving like other sects under persecution. Most of them are led; so their character is to be taken from that of their leaders. These are, for the most part, men of broken fortunes, and of desperate ambition, and animated by views very different from their professions. To these are joined some, whom a generous and sincere enthusiasm has borne beyond their interest;

irritated perhaps excessively at the indiscriminating intolerance of the alarmists, and zealous in the assertion of some truths, which those with whom they co-operate have used as a decoy. The third order is that of philosophers, and of course very small. These necessarily vary in their maxims and opinions, and only agree in blaming something more or less in both parties, and in endeavouring to reconcile their hostility. We have been disturbed by rumours of conspiracy and intended massacre; certainly exaggerated by the organs of alarm, but probably not destitute of all foundation.

a What activities in 1793 and 1794 in Scotland could be ascribed to the 'desperate democrats'?

b Why were 'rumours of conspiracy and intended massacre' exaggerated?

c Jeffrey presumably considered himself as one of the 'philosophers'. Try to write a description of the political situation in Scotland in 1794 from the point of view of (*i*) an aristocrat, (*ii*) a democrat.

2

Part of a report sent to Henry Dundas in 1795, describing the Lochmaben burgh council:

The present State of the Magistracy and Town-council is as follows:

James Richardson merchant in Lochmaben, holds the Office of Provost, and his Son *Robert* that of Eldest Baillie. They have uniformly been in the Interest of the Duke, and hold several of His Grace's Burgal Lands, which they were favoured with, on account of their friendship to him, and which it would be much against their Interest to lose.

Besides this, at the Time the distress fell upon the Partners of Douglas Heron and Co., of which the Provost was one, the Duke was pleased to interfere, and granted him and his son Robert, a loan; which Saved their Credit, and prevented their Heritable subjects being brought to sale, and, which loan, it is believed, is yet outstanding.

Second Baillie: *Alexander Dickson* Joiner, fills that Office; He was uniformly shown his attachment to the Interest of the Duke, and his son *William* late merchant in Annan, (whose affairs went into confusion) and who is one of the present Members of the Town Council of Lochmaben, as a reward for his Father's Integrity, was put into His Grace's farm of East-riggs in Dornock Barony, and which is the great means of supporting him and his numerous Children. He has not yet obtained a lease of these lands and it is presumed, he and his

Father would not forfeit his Grace's good wishes, by breaking their former professions and going against the Duke's inclinations.

a How did the Duke of Queensberry maintain his control over the various members of the council?

b How could that control have been shaken, if at all?

3

This is a letter written in 1803 to Henry Dundas, Viscount Melville. One of the Scottish peers in the House of Lords had just died and Dundas was asking that Lord Kellie should be elected in his place.

> My Dear Lord,
>   It will afford me great pleasure to give my vote to Lord Kellie.
>   Allow me my Lord to remind you of my Brother *David* an old and deserving Officer, not of a Constitution to risk going to the Indies, but the Command of a recruiting district, is all that is asked for him.
>   I alws̄ am my Dr Lord
>   Your Lops faithfull Etc
>   Leven & Melville

a Why should Lord Leven expect Dundas to help his brother David?

b What would have been the chief difficulties faced by Dundas at election times?

7 Religion and education

At the beginning of the eighteenth century religion played a much more important part in the lives of most people than it does today. Though men and women were no longer killed because they refused to accept the religion laid down by the government, it was still taken for granted that those who rejected the state church might be excluded from certain official posts and be looked on with suspicion by their fellow citizens. Most people therefore went to church regularly and the clergyman, looked up to as a man of importance and learning, played a very large part in the life of the community. This was true of both England and Scotland though the two countries had quite different religious traditions.

Englishmen often found it difficult to understand Scotland's religious history.

> 'It is in vain', wrote the Rev. Sydney Smith in about 1800, 'that I study the subject of the Scotch Church. I have heard it ten times over from Murray, and twenty times from Jeffrey, and I have not the smallest conception what it is about. I know it has something to do with oatmeal, but beyond that I am in utter darkness.'

The Church of England had been made by men who were determined to create an organisation which would be acceptable to the majority of Englishmen and this often involved compromises and vagueness on matters of belief. It was sometimes difficult to find out exactly what the official teaching of the church was. It was essentially a comfortable, reassuring organisation and a cheerful, common-sense, down-to-earth clergyman like Sydney Smith was in some ways a typical product.

The beliefs of the church

The Scottish church, on the other hand, was the product of rebellion. Its fight for existence had begun in the middle of the sixteenth century, and had ended in triumph at the end of the seventeenth when it replaced the Episcopal church as the officially approved state church. Men like to know exactly what they are fighting for. As a result the doctrines of the church were clear and well known. Thus the Scottish church rejected any kind of state control. The church had to be separate from the state, with its own organisation, controlled by a General Assembly elected by congregations who were also to appoint their own parish ministers. The church taught predestination: that is, that God has decreed who should be saved and who should be damned. The former, known as the elect, are assured of a place in paradise, not through their own merits or actions, for no man could ever deserve so much, but only because of God's generosity. The damned, on the other hand, are helpless. No matter what they do they will still be damned because God decreed it before time began. It is perhaps not unfair to say that most members of the church considered themselves among the elect, while many numbered the followers of all other religions among the damned. The church also taught that all Christians were equally able to understand the scriptures and therefore needed no priests to act as interpreters.

Finally, the church laid down a high standard of conduct which it expected its members to follow. It was, moreover, prepared to discipline those who fell short of this standard.

The church after 1689

The church found some difficulty in adjusting to its new official status. For one thing it meant working in partnership with the government and, at parish level, with the local landowners. This involved making compromises and as a rule it was the church which had to give way. This led to much heart searching, for too much compromise could lead to a state-dominated church, which their ancestors had fought to prevent. A critical decision was made in 1712. Before the Presbyterian church took over, it was usual for the local landowners to appoint the parish minister. This right of patronage was taken over by the representatives of the congregation in 1689, but in 1712 it was given back to the original patrons, though the congregations had the right to reject their choice if they wished. As time passed the powers of the patrons tended to increase and those of the congregations to diminish. The General Assembly went so far as to appoint committees to go round helping to induct ministers chosen by the patron in the face of opposition from a large number of the congregation. Sometimes there were riots and troops has to be used.

Some ministers felt very strongly on this matter of patronage. Ebenezer Erskine told the Synod of Perth and Stirling in 1732:

> I can find no warrant from the word of God to confer the spiritual privileges of His house upon the rich beyond the poor; whereas by this Act the man with the gold ring and gay clothing is preferred unto the man with the vile raiment and poor attire.

In 1733 he left the church and set up a separate Associate Presbytery: by 1742 nineteen ministers had joined him. He tended to attract the more severe and uncompromising members of the church and they did not find it easy to work together, to such an extent, indeed, that the Associate Presbytery itself found it impossible to remain united. Its difficulties were, of course, greeted with delight by the Church of Scotland.

A minister's life

Yet the vast majority of the nine hundred parish ministers were too busy with parochial affairs to give much thought to the difficulties of the Associate Presbytery. The average minister worked hard for his money—usually about £40 a year. He had to visit every family in his parish to examine their religious beliefs at certain times each year. Many parishes were very large. Few had good roads. Overnight stops were often necessary on such visits, frequently in dreadful accommodation. Then he had to preside at the kirk session meetings, where the elders enquired into all cases of moral backsliding in the parish. This might involve anything from adultery to uttering some mild oath, and the culprits would be admonished, or fined, or ordered to do public penance before the whole congregation. In addition the minister had regular meetings with his brother ministers in the presbytery at which they might discuss some points of doctrine as well as considering cases referred to them by the kirk sessions. Each Sunday he had to preach and was expected to do so with a display of learning as well as emotion. Sermons were long—often more than an hour—and it was considered wrong to read them. Many ministers tried to heighten their effect by adopting a kind of singsong way of preaching. Some, it was said in 1759, 'in heavy dismal tones draw out words to immoderate length with distortion of face'. There was no escape for the congregation. All had to attend church on Sunday. Absentees were punished, as was any unnecessary activity, such as taking a stroll or grinding snuff.

Occasionally there would be a communion service. These were rare—sometimes there were years between them. The churches

Many Scottish parish churches were either repaired or completely rebuilt between 1780 and 1830. The new buildings were usually plain but substantial.

were small and inconvenient. 'In many parts of Scotland,' wrote one traveller 'our Lord seems still to be worshipped in a stable— and a very wretched one.' It was therefore the custom to hold the communion outside and often to combine forces with other parishes, as had been done in the old days when the Covenanters had met to worship in huge bands in the open. Such enormous meetings were popular but the atmosphere at them became less and less devout as the years passed. At first they were very impressive occasions with much heart searching, but in 1759 an observer wrote of them as 'an absurd mixture of the serious and the comic' with some parsons preaching to small groups, others to larger, jostling crowds of men, at one moment devout and serious, at the next cursing their neighbours for crushing or treading on them. It was difficult to take them seriously any longer and slowly the great meetings were abandoned, for the enthusiasm which was their mainspring was waning.

The Moderates

In fact the church was steadily becoming more worldly. To begin with this may well have been all to the good. The persecuting days were past and visions of Hell and damnation were not really acceptable to the much more confident, go-ahead society which was emerging. It was a good thing that the public humiliation of sinners was stopped. It saved many an infant's life, for mothers of illegitimate children now accepted them, instead of being tempted to avoid public scorn by killing them at birth. There was, too, a much more tolerant attitude to the Sabbath and to such amusements as dancing and play-going. Though there were always a number of 'evangelical' or 'high-flying' ministers who believed firmly in the old values, those ministers who favoured 'moderate' policies came gradually to control the General Assembly.

From 1762 to 1780 their leader was Dr. William Robertson, an honest, intelligent and very realistic man. He encouraged the clergy to look after their parishes properly and to preach thoughtful, sensible sermons. He was pleased, too, when they took an interest in the world of learning. He was himself principal of Edinburgh University. Robertson was upset by suggestions that the church should persecute those who disagreed with its doctrines, for he wished all religious opinions to be tolerated. On the other hand he was pleased if those ministers who disagreed with the Moderates decided to leave the church, for this helped to keep the church itself united and firmly under Moderate control. Thus he made no attempt to persuade Thomas Gillespie and his two colleagues, Thomas Boston and Thomas Colier, to remain in the church when they complained that it was too narrow and exclusive. As a result they founded the Presbytery of Relief in 1761, which grew into a separate Presbyterian church. However, Robertson was very careful to keep the church free from political control.

Decline of the church

The Scottish church under Robertson's control was in many ways an impressive institution. But it was not to last. For one thing, the quality of the clergy began to decline. All over Western Europe religion was being questioned in a fundamental way and some of the most prominent scholars and philosophers were atheists. The same applied in Scotland. David Hume, for instance, was an unbeliever. It was, therefore, no longer taken for granted by all that a career in the church was desirable. In addition, the standard of living of other occupations was rising, so that the position of the clergy in society was lower. A zeal for religion would overcome such obstacles but those with fire in their bellies were put off by the cool reason of Moderatism. Thus the church lost both the intelligent career men and the enthusiasts. It had to make do with the second- or even the third-rate men who seemed to have no grasp of doctrines, whose only aim appeared to be to preach an elegant and inoffensive sermon and keep well in with those with power and influence. The Rev. Gavin Parker heard such a preacher in 1837:

> There was much to please as in a theatre: much to reach the carnal heart: almost nothing of any use to a spiritual mind: much not faithful, not intelligible, not discriminating, not true: much to deceive and to soothe sinners asleep in sin: nothing to alarm.

It was unfortunate that Principal George Hill, who replaced

Principal Robertson
by Sir Joshua Reynolds.

Robertson as leader of the Moderates in 1780, shared the short-comings of many of his party. 'His influence', wrote Henry Cockburn, 'depended on a single power—that of public speaking.' He had none of Robertson's scholarship or foresight, and he allowed the church to drift more and more in the direction of state control until eventually the Moderates came almost wholly under the influence of Henry Dundas and his henchmen. The French Revolution, which seemed to be a great victory for atheism, made many fear for the future of Christianity and in Scotland the church seemed in no shape to fight. In 1796 it rejected the idea of supporting foreign missions and showed no interest in trying to win the support of the workers in Scotland. This work was eventually organised by Robert Haldane, a retired sea-captain, and his brother James, who began going on preaching tours in 1797. In 1798, with the help of a few ministers of the church, they set up the 'Society for Propagating the Gospel at Home' and, enlisting the help of an English preacher, Rowland Hill, went on another tour in 1799. They were hindered by the opposition of the majority of the clergy and Rowland Hill published blistering attacks on the attitude of the church to their work. The groups founded by the Haldanes therefore stayed separate from the church and formed the foundation of most of the Baptist and Congregationalist bodies in Scotland.

After the war interest in religion tended to increase. Disbelief and atheism were no longer popular, being too closely identified with the excesses of the French Revolution. This renewal of interest was in itself a challenge to the church, for by now the outlook of most of its ministers was too secular to be in tune with any spirit of religious revival. The Rev. Gavin Parker was one of the exceptions, and in his diary he was unsparing in his criticism of his easy-going colleagues. 'Their knowledge of doctrine', he wrote, 'is vague, idefinite, general.' Again, 'They are so much addicted to laughing and jesting when talking about religion and religious opinions, that I fear there is very little heart-work in their religion.' Finally, 'They seem very unthankful for any friendly hints regarding their deficiencies.' No doubt Parker was self-righteous and irritating, but he knew what he believed and preached it clearly. The trouble was that the control of the church was in the hands of men who had lost touch with the spirit of Presbyterianism to such an extent that they were capable of actions directly opposed to its basic beliefs. Hence the great disruption of 1843.

Other sects

There were other sects apart from the church and its offshoots. The Episcopal church still survived in spite of some persecution. They were traditionally Jacobite, but accepted the Hanoverian succession in 1788 and were officially tolerated after 1792. Scotland was divided into dioceses, each with its own bishop, and the Episcopalians began to win converts among the upper classes. The reverse was true of the Catholics. They, too, were persecuted after 1745, for their main strength was in the Highlands. Many emigrated, even though all legislation against them was repealed in 1793. Their numbers began to increase after 1800 when many Irishmen came to the Lowland industrial centres.

Parochial schools

Methodism never really caught on in Scotland. Wesley said it was because the Scots 'knew too much'—a kind of back-handed compliment to the Scottish education system, which was, indeed, a source of some pride. Since Protestantism taught that every Christian had the right to interpret the Bible for himself, it was clearly important that all should be taught to read. Accordingly at the Reformation an attempt had been made to set up a nation-wide system of education, and with the triumph of Presbyterianism at the end of the seventeenth century an act of 1696 once again tried to establish universal state education. In each parish the heritors had to provide a school house and a salary of between a hundred and two hundred marks a year for a teacher. If the heritors failed to do this, then the local presbytery could request the commissioners of supply to do the job instead.

So much for the law. It is difficult to say how far it was effec-tive. It used to be maintained that it was largely ignored, but historians are now not so sure. In compact, prosperous Lowland parishes the inhabitants were made to pay their share, the school house was built and a teacher employed at the full legal salary, teaching the children of all the parish, laird and tenant alike. But in other places there might be no school house and insufficient money to pay a full salary. In 1772 the kirk session of Strath-blane spoke of the school as being 'tossed from barn to barn' until the schoolmaster paid rent for a house out of his own salary, which amounted in all to only £4 a year, while at Lintrathen, according to the *Statistical Account*, the schoolmaster's salary 'is 6 or 4 bolls of meal, to be collected from the tenants; while the hut he occupies is hardly fit for the meanest beggar'.

None the less, by 1760 most Lowland parishes probably had a school of some sort, but this was not the end of the problem. Many parishes were too large or too populous for the school to be adequate. To overcome this, 'adventure schools' were sometimes set up. These were small private schools financed entirely from the fees charged by the teacher, who was frequently less well qualified than those in the official parish schools. They taught reading and writing, but little more, and if the parish minister disapproved of

A parish school built after the 1803 act. The school rooms are downstairs. The teacher's flat is upstairs and can only be reached by an iron staircase at the back of the building.

them, then he could have them closed down. Yet if all the children had gone to school all the time, parish school and adventure school alike would have been overwhelmed by the numbers in many parishes. Some pupils did attend continuously for five or six years. But others went only for a year or so. Others frequently stayed away for long periods when there was work for them to do on the farm or at home. Some never went to school at all.

In the Highlands the problems were much greater. Highland parishes were commonly too large and the population too scattered for one school to be much use. In such cases the teacher sometimes moved from place to place. Sometimes there were several little schools, each wretched and with a very badly paid teacher. Sometimes there was no teacher and no school.

At all events there was a good deal of dissatisfaction with the state of affairs, particularly in the Highlands where many of the clansmen were totally illiterate. They were frequently Catholic as well. The conscience of the Protestant Lowlands was stirred, and in 1708 the 'Scottish Society for Propagating Christian Knowledge' was set up in Edinburgh. Its aim was to found schools to teach English, arithmetic and church music. But it had to be careful, for if it showed itself willing to finance schools in parishes where none existed, then the heritors in such parishes would be relieved of their legal responsibilities and of the expense involved. The society therefore made a rule that it would only set up schools in those parishes where there was already a parish school with a fully paid teacher. It thus confined its activities to those large parishes where one school was insufficient. The work was difficult. There were too few Gaelic-speaking teachers, communications were bad and the clansmen and their chiefs were frequently indifferent if not hostile. But gradually, especially after 1750, progress was made, for, as well as building its own schools, the society was constantly putting pressures on the heritors of parishes without schools to provide them as the law laid down.

The schoolmasters

Yet problems remained. Where the heritors failed to provide schools, the commissioners of supply often found it impossible as well, for they simply could not get the inhabitants to pay. Meanwhile teachers in most parishes were discontented with their lot. In 1782 they drew up a memorial:

> 'Ninety years', they wrote, 'have produced such a change and so great an improvement in agriculture, navigation, commerce, arts and riches of the country that £15 sterling per annum at the end of the last century may be considered a better income than £45 at the present time. Suppose then that in Scotland there are 900 parochial schoolmasters, which is near the truth, 800 of them will be found struggling with indigence, inferior in point of income to 800 day labourers in the best cultivated parts of the Island and receiving one half of the emoluments of the menial servants of country gentlemen.'

It became difficult to fill vacancies, and in 1803 parliament acted, increasing the salary of teachers to between three hundred and four hundred marks and laying down that they were entitled to a two-roomed house, with a quarter of an acre for garden—all to be provided by the heritors. Large parishes were empowered to provide for two schools. The act was not generous, but it was after all passed when Britain was fighting for her existence against Napoleon and at a time when many felt that to educate ordinary children might only lead them to question their position in society and demand awkward 'rights'.

The education offered by the parish school varied from place to place and from time to time according to the ability of the teacher. All taught their pupils to read. All taught them their catechism and made sure that they were familiar with the Bible. Some did much more, teaching their charges arithmetic, literature and sometimes even a smattering of Latin and French. At worst they offered an education of sorts equally to all social classes which was unknown in most European countries. The fees for such a schooling amounted to about 2s a quarter—though they rose after 1803. The children of the poor were taught free.

Burgh schools

In the towns education was controled by the burgh councils which set up schools that concentrated on teaching Latin. The plan of education at one such, Aberdeen Grammar School, was thus described in 1820:

> The boys are generally five years at this school. In the first year they are grammatically taught the elements of the Latin language from Ruddiman's Rudiments. After having made some progress therein, they learn Watt's Vocabulary, all the nouns of which they are made to decline, with adjectives; and when they have made sufficient advances in the elements, they read and explain the first six colloquies of Corderius, and a sacred lesson from the Rudimenta Pictatis. During the first quarter of this course, they are exercised, one hour in the morning, in reading English.
>
> On their promotion to the second class, they are employed at the Grammatical Exercises, which they turn into Latin, and write a version from that book three times a week: at the same time continuing to read and translate Corderius. They are also

instructed in the rules for the genders of nouns, and for the con-
jugation of verbs, from Watt's Grammar. Towards the latter
part of the year, they read and translate Cornelius Nepos.

In the third year, they continue to read, for some time,
Cornelius Nepos, as before, and then proceed to Caesar's
Commentaries. Having gone through the Grammatical
Exercises a second time, they are taught to construct the
sentences in Mair's Introduction, and that is continued through
the fourth and fifth classes. For a sacred lesson, they read and
translate Castalio's Dialogues; and, towards the end of the year,
having committed to memory the rules of prosody contained in
Watt's Grammar, they read Ovid's Metamorphoses, and are
instructed to scan every lesson, and to apply the rules of
prosody.

In the fourth and fifth classes, under the rector, they read and
translate Caesar, Sallust, Livy, Cicero, Virgil, and Horace;
and, for a sacred lesson, Buchanan's Psalms. They are not only
taught to scan every lesson which they read in the works of the
poets, but commit the most of their lessons to memory. When
any allusion, either to antiquities, geography, or to mythology,
occurs in these lessons, it is carefully explained to them by the
rector; and, that they may be made fully acquainted with those
studies, the proper books are recommended for their perusal.
They also read one of Terence's comedies, which the scholars,
in ancient times, were in the use of rehearsing, annually, in the
public hall; but that practice has been in disuse for upwards of
forty years.

The scholars, in the third, fourth, and fifth classes, have pre-
scribed to them, thrice a week, by their respective masters,
exercises of a few English sentences, which they turn into Latin;
their versions being exhibited on Saturday forenoon, and carefully examined. They are also occasionally exercised in making
English versions from the Latin classics.

Changes in schools

This was clearly a very narrow education and Aberdeen Grammar
School was really rather out of date, for by 1800 many such

schools had begun teaching modern languages, rules for finding areas and volumes, and even logarithms. There was certainly a demand for these subjects, and for others like science and commerce which would be of practical use for the pupils in their careers. In some places, to make more money, the schoolmaster taught such extra subjects in his spare time, but a number of burghs set up new schools called writing or commercial schools to fill this need. In other places academies were set up, financed by private subscription. These were usually outside the control of the burgh council, and taught mostly science subjects. The first was founded in Perth in 1761, and by 1802 there were similar schools in Dundee, Inverness, Elgin, Fortrose, Ayr and Dumfries. Parents who wished their sons to receive a practical education would send them to an academy in preference to a university. Edinburgh Academy, founded in 1824, was different. In the first place, it was to teach Latin and Greek, and, in the second, it was intended for 'the better class of boys'. Perhaps this was to try to stem the flow of well-to-do boys who were sent by their parents to the English public schools to acquire the background, the accent and the friends to help them succeed in careers in England. If this was the case, it failed. Most of the new town schools catered for middle-class children. Working-class children were rarely catered for properly. This was particularly true in the growing industrial towns where many of the population were immigrants. It was, in the nature of things, difficult to provide schools to keep pace with the mushroom growth of such towns, but even where schools were built it was often not easy to get the children to attend them. In the first place there was often work for them in the factories, but in addition many of the Highland and Irish workers were Catholic and refused to send their children to schools which were dominated by the Church of Scotland. Many were therefore illiterate.

Education for girls

For girls any sort of higher education was out of the question. They needed only to learn to run a household and, if they were rich, to amuse themselves and their husbands. The very rich had governesses. The middle classes might well send their daughters to

This engraving by David Allan shows the laying of the foundation stone of the New College in Edinburgh in 1789. The professors and students stand on the left. The Lord Provost and the council are on the right. Standing in front of the stone is the Grand Master Mason of Scotland.

a school like that advertised in the *Aberdeen Journal* in 1774 in the following terms:

Miss Rankens, Boarding School Mistresses in the Shiprow Return their most grateful Thanks to all those who have been pleased to favour them with the Charge of their Daughters either as Boarders or Day-scholars, and hope for the continuance of their Friendship. They have this Year found it necessary to enlarge their House considerably, and for the still greater Advantage of the young Ladies under their Care Miss Katie has been for several months this Winter at Edinburgh, improving herself in the newest methods of the following Articles and will teach them at the most reasonable Rates, Viz. Embroidery on Silk and Cloth; embroidering Buttons for Mens Cloaths and Ladies Riding habits: working Lace; Shading in the Tambour on Silk, Muslin and Gauze, interspersed with

Silver or Gold; Open Stitch on the Tambour with the two-
pointed Needle, painting different Kinds; Japanning on Silk;
new Sprigs, Pongs, and breast Flowers. Agreements may be
made from the Country by Letter address'd as above.

Universities

Scotland was well provided with universities. There was one each
at St. Andrews, Glasgow and Edinburgh and two at Aberdeen.
Like the parish schools they educated all social classes. Course
fees were about £2 a year. In 1774 Dr. Johnson was told that a
student could get board and education at St. Andrews for £10 a
year. Many of the students reduced even this sum by seeking out
the cheapest lodgings—perhaps £1 a year—and bringing their own
bag of oatmeal for food. The quality of education was not, at first,
very high. The universities had been given little peace in the
seventeenth century, for as each religious faction seized power in
the state, so they got rid of all those who opposed them in the
universities. Thus the colleges were dominated by religious strife
and had little time left for learning. In any case the system of
tuition made any advanced study difficult, as each group of
students was taken through the whole course by the same regent,
whose knowledge of parts of it might be anything but perfect.
The students were very young—mostly in their early teens. The
medium of instruction was Latin. Thus Scottish universities, like
those in England, entered the eighteenth century in very poor
order. But, unlike the English, they made great strides forward.

Several factors helped to account for this. Under the Moderates
there was a greater degree of religious toleration than formerly
and in any case the power of the church over the universities was
less. Thus John Leslie, a man whose religious views were suspect,
was appointed professor of mathematics at Edinburgh in spite of
the opposition of the Moderates in 1805. The language of instruction was changed to English and the system of regents was
abolished, so that by 1800 the students were taught each subject
by the professor of that subject. This put a great responsibility on
the shoulders of the individual professor. Their salaries were up to

£100 a year and had to be made up by the fees they collected from their students. Even so, some rarely if ever lectured, but others were not only learned men but also enthusiastic teachers. Such men brought fame to their colleges and also grew rich. Thus John Millar, professor of civil law at Glasgow from 1761 to 1801, attracted students from far and wide. Adam Smith, former professor of philosophy at Glasgow, made himself and his university famous in 1776 by publishing *The Wealth of Nations*, one of the most influential books ever written. At Edinburgh a faculty of law and a professorship of history were established. Adam Ferguson, professor of moral philosophy, wrote an *Essay on the History of Civil Society* in 1767, and his successor, Dugald Stewart, lectured so well as to become fashionable while still retaining his scholarship and his dignity.

But Edinburgh's chief claim to fame was her school of medicine, which was certainly the best in the United Kingdom. Monro, professor of anatomy, got on well with the city authorities, and co-operated with them in founding the Royal Infirmary in 1746, which gave the students practical experience of hospital work. Two first-rate professors, Cullen and Black, came from Glasgow, and by 1800 Edinburgh's medical school was turning out fifty doctors a year, was famous all over Europe, and had given Scottish doctors the reputation which they still enjoy today.

There were, of course, still blemishes. One of the reasons why Black and Cullen left Glasgow was that there was much petty intrigue and back-biting among the professors there. At Aberdeen some progress was made, but much time and energy was spent in quarrels between the two universities. Attempts to unite them only made matters worse. But it was at St. Andrews that least was done. Principal Hill, leader of the Moderates in the General Assembly, seemed to make little effort to put an end to the corruption and idleness which was sapping all the college's strength. It is perhaps typical that at a time when Edinburgh's medical degrees were universally respected, St. Andrews was prepared to sell the degree of MD for ready cash, even though it had no medical school. It would be a pity to end the chapter on this note, for St. Andrews was not typical. By 1800 the Scottish universities certainly offered a much better education than either Oxford or

Cambridge, and many Englishmen came north to benefit from it.

So much, then, for Scotland's churches and her educational institutions. The church was in a critical state, having lost a number of its members in its efforts to come to terms with its 'official' status. Nor were its troubles over. On the educational front progress had been made, but the school system was barely coping with the increasing population and was threatening to break down completely in the new industrial towns.

Documents

1 *The induction*

This is an extract from *Annals of the Parish*, a novel by John Galt about a clergyman's life in a country parish. Here he writes about his induction to his parish which is set in 1760:

> I was put in by the patron, and the people knew nothing whatsoever of me, and their hearts were stirred into strife on the occasion, and they did all that lay within the compass of their power to keep me out, insomuch, that there was obliged to be a guard of soldiers to protect the presbytery; and it was a thing that made my heart grieve when I heard the drum beating and the fife playing as we were going to the kirk. The people were really mad and vicious, and flung dirt upon us as we passed, and reviled us all, and held out the finger of scorn at me; but I endured it with a resigned spirit, compassionating their wilfulness and blindness. Poor old Mr. Kilfuddy of the Brachill got such a clash of glar on the side of his face, that his eye was almost extinguished.
>
> When we got to the kirk door, it was found to be nailed up, so as by no possibility to be opened. The sergeant of the soldiers wanted to break it, but I was afraid that the heritors would grudge and complain of the expense of a new door, and I supplicated him to let it be as it was: we were, therefore, obligated to go in by a window, and the crowd followed us in the most unreverent manner, making the Lord's house like an inn on a fair day, with their grievous yellyhooing. During the time of the psalm and the sermon, they behaved themselves better, but when the induction came on, their clamour was dreadful.

Galt's account is from the point of view of the minister. Try writing one from the point of view of a member of the crowd, justifying the action you are taking.

2 *'The Holy Fair'*

In this poem Burns wrote of the huge communion gatherings:

> The lads and lasses, blythely bent
>   To mind baith saul an' body,
> Sit round the table, weel content,
>   An' steer about the toddy.
> On this ane's dress, an' that ane's leuk,
>   They're makin' observations;
> While some are cosy i' the neuk,
>   An' formin' assignations
>   To meet some day.
>
> But now the Lord's ain trumpet touts,
>   Till a' the hills are rairin'
> An' echoes back return the shouts;
>   Black Russel is na sparin':
> His piercing words, like Highlan' swords,
>   Divide the joints an' marrow;
> His talk o' Hell, where devils dwell,
>   Our very 'sauls does harrow'
>   Wi' fright that day!
>
> A vast, unbottom'd, boundless pit,
>   Fill'd fou o' lowin' brunstane,
> Wha's ragin' flame, an' scorchin' heat,
>   Wad melt the hardest whun-stane!
> The half-asleep start up wi' fear
>   An' think they hear it roarin',
> When presently it does appear
>   'Twas but some neebor snorin'
>   Asleep that day.

a What shows that 'Black Russel' was an old-fashioned preacher?

b How would a Moderate have preached?

c What features of Holy Fairs presented in this poem were un-
   desirable?

3 *The academies*

Part of a report made to Perth Town Council in 1760 by the Rev. James
Bonnar who had been asked to advise them on Education:

   Thus in times long past, all learning was made to consist in the grammatical knowledge of dead languages, and skill in metaphysical subtleties, while what had an immediate reference to life and practice was despised. But providence has cast our lot in happier times, when things begin to be valued according to their use, and men of the greatest abilities have employed their skill in making the sciences contribute not only to the improvement of the physician, lawyer, and divine, but to the improvement of the merchant, mechanic, and farmer, in their respective arts.

a What sort of school and curriculum resulted from the view of learning 'in times long past'?

b Detail the changes which came as a result of the new attitude.

8 The golden age

The late eighteenth and early nineteenth centuries are often regarded as a golden age in Scotland's history, principally because in these years the country made enormous material progress and seemed to have more than its fair share of talented men in most fields. For a time, indeed, Edinburgh was regarded by many as the intellectual capital of Britain. Yet it was not so many years before that Boswell had felt it necessary to apologise to Johnson because he came from Scotland. How had this change come about?

In the first place, after 1750 Scotland was a secure place in which to live. The Union with England was taken for granted and the Highlands were under firm government control. Raids and rebellions were clearly things of the past and men could turn the whole of their energy into peaceful, constructive channels. This was in marked contrast to earlier periods in Scotland's history. But rebellions were not the only, or even the most important, threat to which Scots had been exposed in the past. Far more significant for most had been a constant grinding struggle against poverty, disease and, in some cases, starvation. Improvements in farming methods introduced during the eighteenth century meant that most Scots now always had enough food and a standard of housing far superior to that endured by their ancestors. They were therefore fitter, more energetic and more optimistic. This improvement was not peculiar to Scotland, but it was much more dramatic here than in most countries.

Next, narrow, intolerant and ferocious religious bickering was on the decline. In the seventeenth century this had sometimes reached hysterical proportions and had been allied with primitive superstitions and the persecution of witches. It was not an atmos-

David Hume dressed in the
height of fashion

phere which encouraged calm reflection or original ideas. But the last execution for witchcraft took place in 1727 and in the eighteenth century people felt much freer to reach unorthodox conclusions and to broadcast them in books and lectures. Moreover, because of her system of schools and universities and an ingrained respect for learning, Scotland was able to take advantage of the new sense of security and optimism and produced a steady stream of scholars, craftsmen and artists.

Scottish scholars

Since Scotland's society was changing so quickly, it is not surprising that some of her best scholars turned their attention to the way in which societies developed, and how they should be governed. Both Robertson, who wrote three major historical works including a history of Scotland, and Hume saw history as a means of finding these things out, and Hume in particular was contemptuous of English historians, whose attitude he thought unscholarly. He would, he said, as soon expect to find a serious historian in Lapland as in England. This demand for a serious examination of the nature of human society led to Adam Ferguson's *Essay on the History of Civil Society,* to Adam Smith's work on political economy and, at a different level, found expression in Sir John Sinclair's zeal for collecting statistical information. If men could learn how society worked, then they would, it was thought, be well on the way to controlling its growth and development.

But not all Scottish thinkers were only interested in political philosophy. In 1783 the Royal Society of Edinburgh was founded to discuss matters of more general interest and Hume himself wrote a *Treatise of Human Nature* in which he tried to revolutionise the traditional outlook on all knowledge. He had no time for religion and his work forced other philosophers to think out their ideas afresh. Most did not agree with him and the result was a controversy which excited wide interest in philosophy. Later Dugald Stewart's lectures both fed and fanned this interest and educated Scots became celebrated for their delight in philosophical back-chat. In some ways this harked back to the days of hair-splitting arguments over religious doctrines, but the subject matter was now more likely to be secular. For instance, the contributors to the *Edinburgh Review* frequently indulged their taste for philosophical speculation in their articles. This sometimes distressed their fellow contributor Sydney Smith, who preferred a lighter touch.

Poets

Yet most Scotsmen, however proud they might have been of the fame of their great scholars, were not really touched by them. They were much more likely to wax enthusiastic over the poetry of Robert Fergusson and Robert Burns. Fergusson lived and died in Edinburgh. His Scots verse was gay and compelling but the range of subject matter was narrow. In some poems he shows a passionate love of his native country, but he wrote mostly about festive occasions in his home town. He lived life to the full and died in 1774 at the age of twenty-four. Burns on the other hand was clearly a great poet. He, too, could celebrate merry-making with verve and abandon, but he could also do much more. He wrote a splendid ballad—*Tam O'Shanter.* He could, when he chose, write biting satires. He could give commonplace events a universal significance, and he wrote some of the finest songs ever written. His touch deserted him only when he tried to write in English, abandoning the dialect of the Ayrshire peasants among whom he had grown up. His poetry then became second-rate, forced and stilted.

Burns's poetry was enormously popular. It was essentially Scottish, yet it was also gay, confident and free, reflecting the prosperous optimistic society which was developing. He had many imitators but no successor, for within a few years of his death in 1796 the language in which he wrote no longer came naturally to educated Scots. They had been taught, all too successfully, to purge their speech and writing of every Scotticism. Even Sir Walter Scott, who could write convincing prose dialogue in Scots, failed when he tried it in verse. Not that much of his verse, although popular in its day, is thought highly of now. He must stand or fall as a novelist, a writer as deeply affected by the great changes he saw going on round him as were Hume or Burns. Scott was profoundly upset by many of these changes, particularly by the growth of a working class which was demanding its rights. He therefore tended to write about the past, which he re-created with vividness, compassion and sometimes a certain envy. His books sold in vast numbers. He was the most popular novelist in Britain. Like Burns he had many imitators but his best work stands head and shoulders above theirs.

Painters

In the eighteenth century Scotland also had more than her fair share of painters. The greatest was probably Henry Raeburn who painted memorable portraits of many prominent men of his day, but Allan Ramsay also painted many fine portraits, while David Allan highlighted the character of country society in such paintings as 'The Penny Wedding'. Sir David Wilkie began in much the same way and became enormously popular in London. In his later years his style changed and he was much patronised by the Royal family. All these men were in the front rank of British artists of their day. Yet they came from a country which had

Raeburn's self-portrait.

scarcely produced a single artist of real merit in the whole of the seventeenth century. Perhaps this flowering of talent was partly due to the general increase in prosperity in Scotland, for this meant that there were enough rich men to give budding artists some hope that they might find patrons to employ them.

Architects

The same was no doubt true of architects. The late eighteenth and early nineteenth centuries were a great age for building in Scotland. Many landowners used the profits from agricultural improvement to rebuild their houses in a more splendid style than before. It was also a time when many towns and villages were either totally rebuilt or greatly extended. Clearly conditions were right for architects to make their names. The most famous were the Adam family. William Adam designed many fine houses, the most ambitious being Hopetoun House in West Lothian. His work was

Robert Adam's design for the front of the New College in Edinburgh.

important, but his son Robert created a style of building and decoration which put him right at the top of his profession. In Edinburgh his work survives in the Old College, the Register House and Charlotte Square, but most of his building was done in England. The same is true of his brother James and of Sir William Chambers who designed Somerset House in London. Though the rewards available in Scotland had increased they still could not match those in England.

Engineers

Many engineers also came from Scotland. James Watt worked out his first improvement to Newcomen's atmospheric engine in conjunction with Professor Black at Glasgow University, and went on to pioneer developments in bleaching as well as surveying canals. William Murdoch pioneered the manufacture of coal gas. Rennie, Bell and, of course, Telford were all Scots. So was John

MacAdam, who was to discover a new, cheaper method of making roads just as effective as Telford's. Once again much of their greatest work was done outside Scotland, but their home country benefited too. Their engines, ships, canals, roads and bridges all helped to increase the general prosperity and enhance the reputation of Scotland.

Town planning

But perhaps the most obvious symbol of the new Scotland was the new town of Edinburgh, built on the other side of the Nor Loch and connected with the old town by two roads only. It was a different world from the old teeming, stinking city crammed together on the Castle rock. The streets were wide, with elegant squares and fine houses. It was a town designed for a genteel and civilised life, and by 1800 the middle and upper classes had moved from the insanitary wynds and closes of the old town to the charm and spaciousness of the new. In spite of having to cope with motor traffic, for which it was never designed, and in spite, too, of some unimaginative commercial development, the new town of Edinburgh is still one of the finest examples of city planning in existence. Many harsh things have, quite rightly, been said about the corrupt and selfish council which ruled Edinburgh in the eighteenth century. But in pressing on with the building of the new town they bankrupted the city in a good cause.

The fame of Edinburgh spread. Other towns in Scotland attempted, in their own way, to match the capital's achievement. For instance the Aberdeen burgh council made that splendid thoroughfare, Union Street, and planned a layout of streets and squares to lie behind it. Unlike the Edinburgh council, however, they went bankrupt before the plan could be executed and only a few fragments remain. Englishmen, too, heard of Edinburgh and of the cultivated and vigorous society which was developing in Scotland. Many came up to see for themselves, and, when the war with France closed the continent to English visitors, the numbers coming to Scotland increased enormously. Under this impact Edinburgh became steadily less and less provincial and Scottish society more sure of itself. Their country, once so despised, had become in a way a centre for pilgrimage, a place to come to complete one's education.

The changed society

The war had other effects too. There had always been a tendency for Scots to go abroad to make their fortunes, and in the eighteenth century many had gone to the West Indies or to India itself. Some came back to Scotland to retire and a few, like Silver of Netherley, spent large sums of money improving their estates. They also brought back new ideas and different ways of life. But during the war with France more Scots than ever before joined the forces and were drafted overseas. Most came back, and their experiences must have led to a questioning of traditional values and a less restricted view of life at all levels of society.

This is not to say that life everywhere in Scotland was wonderful. There was a real cloud behind the silver lining. The old city of Edinburgh still stood, and, populated by the poorer classes, tended to degenerate into slums. Everywhere the population was increasing. In 1707 it probably stood at about 1 000 000. In 1755 it numbered 1 250 000. By 1820 it stood at just over 2 000 000. This rise can be accounted for by better diet, better living conditions and especially by the elimination of smallpox, a disease which had regularly killed a significant proportion of the child population before the adoption of inoculation and vaccination in the latter part of the eighteenth century. In most places the increase in wealth more than kept pace with the growth in population. But this was not the case in the Highlands where there was much misery and degradation. Nor was all well in the new industrial towns where the population, swollen by immigrants from the Highlands and from Ireland, had grown too fast for the authorities to keep pace.

No society ever solves all its problems, and it is only right to point to those which were developing in Scotland at the beginning of the nineteenth century. It would, however, be wrong to overemphasise them, because Scotland had progressed remarkably over the past sixty years. She was richer than she had ever been and had rightly gained the respect of other countries for the learning and ingenuity of her scholars, artists and engineers. Perhaps most important of all, this situation was reflected in a new-found confidence and optimism. It was this which inspired the building of the new town of Edinbugh, the making of the Caledonian Canal, the draining of the moss of Kincardine, the building of the cotton mills and much else. An enormous amount was achieved in a short time by a small country. How does our own age measure up?

Document

An account of Edinburgh matters in about 1780, as remembered by Henry Cockburn:

Two vices especially, which have been long banished from all respectable society, were very prevalent, if not universal, among the whole upper ranks—swearing and drunkenness. Nothing was more common than for gentlemen who had dined with ladies, and meant to rejoin them, to get drunk. To get drunk in a tavern seemed to be considered as a natural, if not an intended consequence of going to one. Swearing was thought the right, and the mark, of a gentleman. And, tried by the test, nobody could now be made to believe how many gentlemen there were. Not that people were worse tempered then than now. They were only coarser in their manners, and had got into a bad style of admonition and dissent. And the evil provoked its own continuance; because nobody who was blamed cared for the censure, or understood that it was serious unless it was clothed in execration. The naval chaplain justified his cursing the sailors, because it made them listen to him; and Braxfield apologised to a lady whom he damned at whist for bad play, by declaring he had mistaken her for his wife. This odious practice was applied with particular offensiveness by those in authority towards their inferiors.

a What other changes had taken place in manners, speech and living conditions for the 'upper ranks' of Edinburgh society apart from those outlined by Cockburn?

b Do you think that there were any ways in which the old fashions were preferable to those which replaced them?

Suggestions for further reading

A. D. Cameron's *Living in Scotland 1760–1820* (Oliver and Boyd) is a very useful collection of documentary extracts on the period.

The following titles in Longman's *Then and There* series are relevant. They lack indexes, which can be inconvenient.

Glasgow and the Tobacco Lords by Norman Nichol
Edinburgh in its Golden Age by W. K. Ritchie
A Border Woollen Town in the Industrial Revolution by Karen McKechnie
Scotland in the Days of Burns by Hyman Shapiro.

In addition all schools ought to be able to obtain copies of entries in the *Old Statistical Account* relating to local parishes. These are likely to be of interest and value.

At a more advanced level T. C. Smout's *History of the Scottish People* (Collins) is the most approachable work. Each chapter has notes on further reading for those who may require more detail still.

Two titles in Evans's *History at Source* series contain much relevant illustrative material. They are:

Scotland: The Rise of Cities 1694–1905 by Alasdair Hogg
Scotland: Revolution in Industry 1703–1913 by Alasdair Hogg

Glossary

(The author would welcome suggestions for additions to this list.)

Balks. Banks of uncultivated ground which separated the ploughed rigs in the run-rig system of farming.

Baron court. A court in which a landowner had the right to try his tenants.

Bear or bere. A hardy but poor-yielding kind of barley.

Bog fir. Remains of pine trees found preserved in peat bogs.

Byre. A cowhouse.

Calvinism. A system of religious belief and church organisation on Presbyterian lines, laid down by John Calvin in Geneva in the sixteenth century.

Capon. A castrated cockerel.

Carding. Combing out cloth fibres to make them fit for spinning.

Cess. A tax which was payable by landowners.

Commissioners for forfeited estates. A body of men appointed by the government to administer the estates confiscated from those found guilty of taking part in the 1745 rebellion. The estates were efficiently administered and returned to their rightful owners in 1784.

Creel. A large wicker basket.

Episcopal church. A church governed by bishops.

Fallow. Land left uncropped to recover its fertility.

Feu. A piece of land held in return for performing duties or paying cash. Sometimes used to mean the terms imposed by a landowner on his tenants.

Fire-damp. Also known as marsh gas (CH_4). An explosive gas found in coal mines and around stagnant pools.

Hagg. In the context probably means 'head of'.

Heritable subjects. Possessions which a man has either inherited or has the right to bequeath.

Heritor. An owner of land.

Hesp. A quantity of linen yarn (*see also* 'Old Scottish measures' at the end of this glossary).

Japanned. Varnished with a hard black gloss.

Kinning lome. A kind of loom.

Kirk session. A court composed of the minister and elders of a parish.

Lairs. Hollows.

Lint. Flax prepared for spinning.

Mortifications. Property left to the church for charitable use.

Moss. A peat bog.

Ox. A castrated bull used for farm work.

Pong. Soft unbleached Chinese silk.

Presbyterianism. A system of church government in which the congregation in each parish appoints its own minister who together with the *elders* make up the *kirk session*, which controls the religious life of the parish and appoints the elders. The ministers and senior elders of neighbouring parishes make up the local *presbytery*, which is the next highest court. The presbyteries send representatives to the *synod*, which controls a number of presbyteries, and to the *General Assembly* of the church which meets every year. In 1800 Scotland had 893 parishes, 78 presbyteries and 15 synods.

Quarter. (*i*) Of animals, one of the four parts into which a carcass was divided.

(*ii*) As a unit of measure for grain, a quarter contained eight bushels and usually weighed about five hundredweight.

Royal burgh. A burgh granted a charter by the crown. Only royal burghs had any right to be represented in parliament.

Saw-tooth gin. A machine to remove the seeds from raw cotton.

Sequestrate. To confiscate possessions to pay a debt.

Shell marl. A mixture of clay and animal shells.

Slough. A hole in a road filled with wet mud.

Statute labour. The work that all the inhabitants of a parish were bound by law to do on the roads each year.

Stott. A young cow or ox.

Superiority. The right to grant feus.

Tack. The period of a lease.

Tacksman. A man who leases a large piece of land from a landowner and then divides it into small farms which he lets to others.

Tambour. A circular frame over which material was stretched for embroidering.

Tied labour. A system whereby the workers cannot change their employment. In eighteenth-century Scotland both miners and salt workers belonged to this category.

Webster. A weaver.

Wedder. A male sheep.

Old Scottish measures

Dry measure

2 pints	=	1 porpet
2 porpets	=	1 peck
4 pecks	=	1 firlot
4 firlots	=	1 boll*

Wet measure

$1\frac{1}{2}$ pints	=	1 choppin
4 choppins	=	1 quart

* A boll of oatmeal weighs about 140 pounds

English equivalents

1 Scottish ell	=	37.2 inches
1 Scottish chain	=	74 feet
1 Scottish acre	=	1.25 English acres

Measure for linen

100 threads	=	1 cut
12 cuts	=	1 hesp
4 hesps	=	1 spindle

Note: actual quantities varied from time to time and from place to place.

Index

(Numbers in italics refer to illustrations.)